QUICK & EASY

MACHINE QUILTS

QUICK & EASY

MACHINE QUILTS

25 MODERN HEIRLOOMS FOR THE HOME

GLORIA NICOL

CREATIVE HOMEOWNER®, Upper Saddle River, New Jersey

First published in 2004 by Cico Books Ltd
32 Great Sutton Street, London EC1V 0NB

Edited by Sarah Hoggett
Photography by Gloria Nicol
Designed by Christine Wood

contents

pillows and table linen

quilts and throws

curtains and cushions

bags and gifts

CHAPTER 1

Pillows and Table Linen

It's amazing how even relatively small items of soft furnishings, such as pillows and place mats, can instantly transform a room—and creating your own, in fabrics that complement the rest of your decorating scheme, is so much more satisfying than buying ready-made ones. Simple machine-quilting is the perfect technique to use to make squishy pillows and softly padded table linen, while patchwork borders and edgings can transform a bland, solid-colored piece into something really special.

PATCHWORK TABLECLOTH
This summer tablecloth, created in myriad pinks and blues, is simple to make and will be surprisingly hardwearing, even with everyday use from the family.

flower-motif pillow

This delightful pillow could grace any room in the home. Shown here in myriad pastel shades of yellow, pink, and lilac, its soft colors look equally stunning on a white or pale summer sofa or as a centerpiece on the bed.

The finished pillow measures 12½ x 16½ inches.

YOU WILL NEED

A selection of fabrics for the patchwork

13¾ x 17¾-inch piece of linen for the pillow front

Small piece of fusible bonding web

13¾ x 17¾-inch piece of interlining

13¾ x 17¾-inch piece of backing fabric

27½-inch length of 1-inch-wide velvet ribbon

Soft embroidery floss and needle

Two 13¾ x 9½-inch pieces of fabric for the pillow back

10-inch zipper

12½ x 16½-inch pillow form

TIPS

- The accuracy of your piecing depends most on cutting the pieces precisely.
- Use a basic straight stitch to sew your pieces together.
- Set the stitch length to 20 per ¼ inch.
- Use a sharp, medium-gauge needle.
- Match the thread type to the fabric type; cotton fabric with cotton or polycotton thread.
- Always piece in the direction of the grain of the fabric.

PRETTY PASTELS
Soft pink and yellow floral prints alternate with solid fabrics in this delicate and feminine-looking pillow.

1 Cut out 2 x 4-inch rectangles from the fabrics selected for the patchwork. You will need approximately 40 pieces. Right sides together, pin and then machine-stitch the strips together along the short edges, taking ½-inch seams, to make long strips. Trim the seams to ¼ inch, and press them flat in one direction.

Cut the strips into lengths 14 inches long so that the seams between the rectangles will be staggered when the strips are joined. Right sides together, machine-stitch the strips down the long edges. Cut another four strips and stitch them together in the same way. Trim the seams to ¼ inch, and press them all in one direction.

2 Place one patchwork piece at each end of the pillow front, matching the edges along the outer edges. Baste the pieces in place.

Using the templates on page 121, make pattern pieces for the flower motif. Choose the three fabrics for the flower motif, and iron fusible bonding web to the back of each one. Cut out all three shapes from the fabrics. Peel the backing from the bonding web on the oval and circle cutout shapes. Place them in position on the outer flower shape so that all the right sides are facing you. Cover with a damp cloth, and iron in place, following the manufacturer's instructions.

Center the whole motif on the pillow front between the patchwork pieces. Remove the backing from the bonding web on the back of the flower; cover with a damp cloth; and iron it in place as before.

3 Place the backing fabric right side down, with the interlining on top of it and the pillow front right side up on top of the interlining. Stitching around the edges, baste the pieces together.

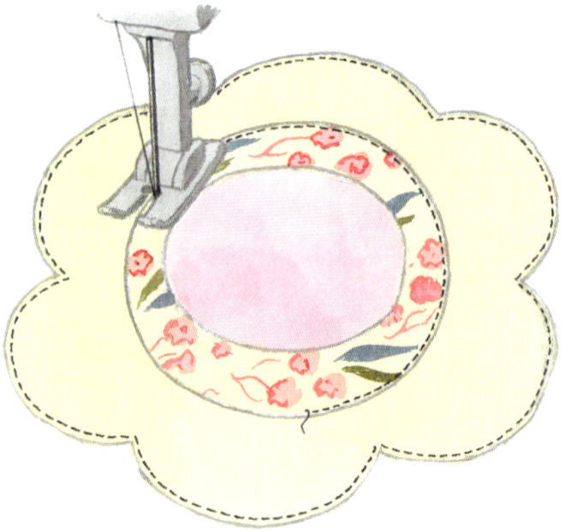

4 Cut the velvet ribbon in half, and place it over the inside edges of the patchwork strips so that it overlaps the seam between the patchwork strip and the pillow front. Topstitch along the long edges of the ribbon and along the seams between each patchwork strip to quilt the layers together. Topstitch around the edges of the flower, oval, and circle, stitching close to the edges.

Using soft embroidery floss, embroider equally spaced double French knots around the oval inside the flower and along the center of the velvet ribbon. (See page 119.) Machine-satin-stitch over the edge of the inside circle. Make up the pillow back, and complete the pillow. (See page 119.)

floral tea cozy

In this pretty pink-and-blue tea cozy, strips cut from an antique table mat, hand-embroidered with satin-stitch flowers, are combined with other strips in solid, period colors to make a piece that is as decorative as it is functional.

In order to hold in the heat, a tea cozy needs to be generously padded—and quilting offers both the necessary insulation as well as infinite decorative possibilities. The piecing is simple: all you need to do is sew strips together until you reach the size you want. You can accentuate the curved shape by sewing a piped edging into the seam or hand-stitching cord in place after you have made the tea cozy.

The tea cozy is 13½ inches wide x 10½ inches high.

YOU WILL NEED

Scraps of fabric for the patchwork

Pattern paper

12 inches of 55-inch-wide batting

24 x 27½ inches of fabric for backing

Ruler

Pencil

Approx. 32 inches of piping

24 x 27½ inches of fabric for lining, in a solid color that matches one of the patchwork colors

Selection of vintage buttons (optional)

Matching sewing threads

FORTIES FANTASIA
Authentic 1940s' fabrics and colors give this tea cozy a charming period feel.

TIP

When you incorporate embroidered fabrics in your patchwork, try to avoid cutting through motifs. You may end up wasting some fabric, but the embroidery will look like an integral part of the design.

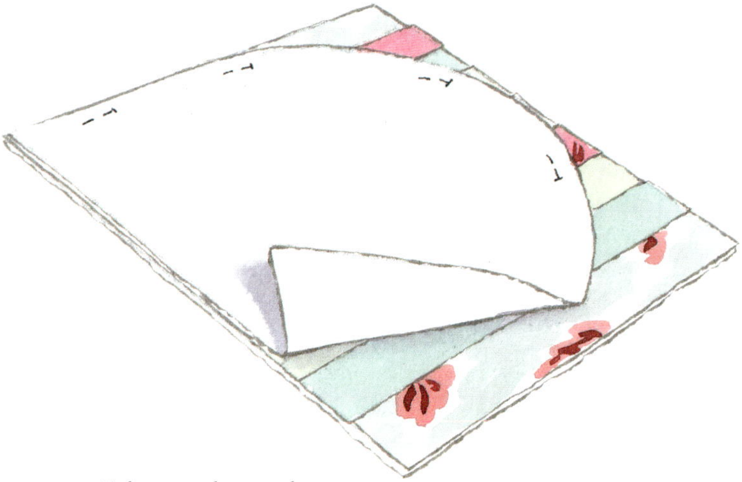

1 Cut 18 12 x 2½-inch strips from the assorted patchwork fabrics. Right sides together and taking ½-inch seams, machine-stitch nine strips together along their long edges to make a rectangle. Press open the seams. Repeat with the remaining nine strips.

2 Enlarge and trace the template on page 120, and make a paper pattern. Cut the batting and backing fabrics in half, widthwise. Place one piece of backing right side down, with the batting on top, and one patchwork rectangle right side up on top of the batting. Pin the pattern to the patchwork, and cut it out, cutting through all three layers. Repeat to make the other side of the tea cozy.

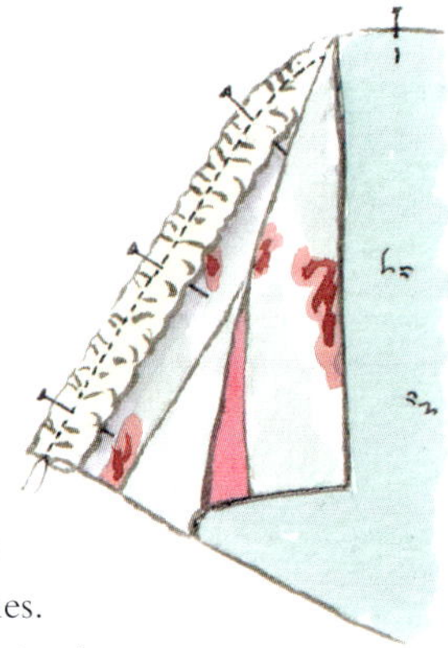

4 Remove the basting stitches. Cut away the batting by ½ inch all around both pieces. Pin the piping along the curved edge of the right side of the tea-cozy front, with the raw edges of the piping facing outward so that the cord is approximately ½ inch from the edge. Right sides together, pin the back and front together. Using the piping foot and taking a ½-inch seam, machine-stitch along the curved edge. Turn right side out.

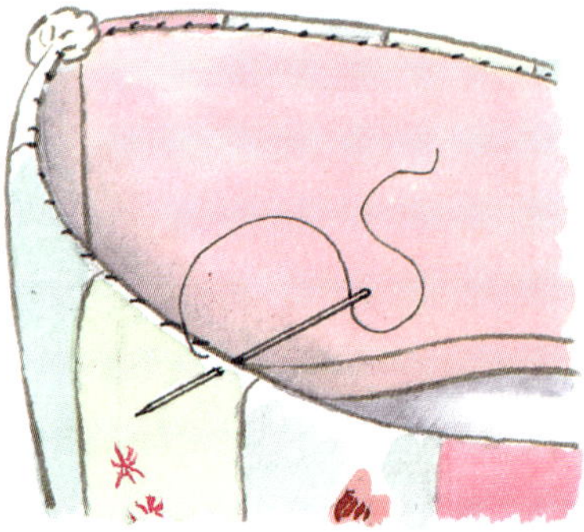

5 Turn under ½ inch along the bottom (straight) edge and baste in place. Using the paper pattern that you made in step 2, cut two pieces from lining fabric. Right sides together, pin and then machine-stitch them along the curved edges. Turn under ½ inch of the lining fabric along the bottom (straight) edge, and press. Push the lining inside the tea cozy, matching the bottom edges, and slip-stitch in place. Stitch buttons onto the tea cozy, stitching through all layers, to secure the lining in place.

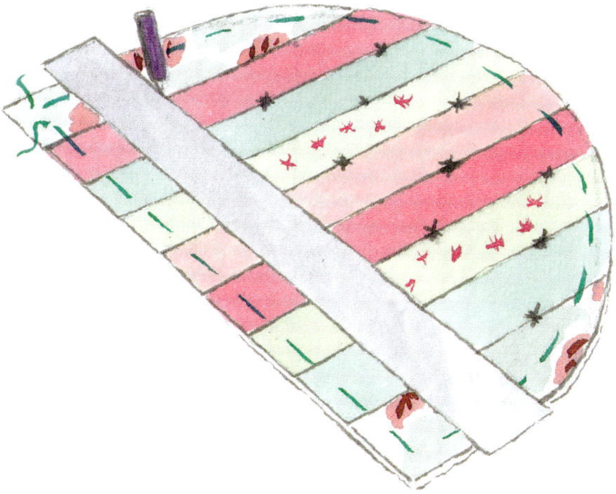

3 Remove the paper pattern, and baste the three layers together. Using a ruler and pencil, mark small dots along the seams of the patchwork at regular intervals. To join the layers together, sew bartacks at these points by setting the stitch to the widest zigzag setting and dropping the feed dog underneath the machine foot. Do this on both sides of the tea cozy.

Vintage buttons sewn onto alternate strips quilt the layers of fabric together and provide a pretty period decoration.

silverware roll

Filled with silverware, or flatware, this quilted roll makes a lovely wedding gift. It is also a stylish and practical way of storing your silverware and helps to stop your best knives and forks from getting scratched and tarnished. The outside of the roll is made from strips of vintage fabrics, contrasting solid colors with a tiny dot design and a classic shirt stripe. Inside are twelve pockets to accommodate several place settings—but you could adjust the number of pockets for keeping individual place settings or simply to hold a whole set of knives.

The finished roll measures 29 x 11 inches when open.

YOU WILL NEED

Sixteen 11 x 2¼-inch pieces cut from at least four fabrics
Lining fabric:
For the main piece: 29 x 11 inches
For the pocket: 22 x 7 inches
For the pocket flap: 21 x 4 inches
Strips of thin silk or cotton cut on the bias, 1 inch wide:
For the main piece: 82 inches
For the pocket: 22 inches
For the flap: 29 inches
For the ties: two pieces each measuring 25 inches

TIPS

- Silverware sizes vary enormously, so before you stitch the individual pockets on the inside of the roll, check that they are going to be wide enough to hold your utensils.
- This is a stylish and practical way of transporting silverware for a picnic.
- Make smaller rolls with six internal pockets so that each roll contains a complete place setting. Positioned on a large plate, they make an attractive table display for an informal lunch party. For a finishing touch, add a centerpiece of flowers in complementary colors.

SIMPLE STYLE
These pretty pastel fabrics complement the tableware to complete this informal table setting. This is a modern take on a traditional idea that is as decorative as it is practical.

log-cabin place mat

This softly padded place mat, constructed from blocks of one of the most popular of all traditional patchwork designs, is a simple but attractive way of protecting your table surface from heat and scratches.

Log-cabin patterns are a useful way of using up small scraps of material. There are many variations, all of which are made by adding strips of fabric around a central square. Using just two fabrics—one light and one dark tone—you can create various effects of light and shade, depending on the placement of the two tones. Here, six identical squares arranged side by side make another repeating pattern.

The finished place mat measures 15½ x 11 inches.

YOU WILL NEED

12-inch square of cream-color linen
13-inch square of floral print
Small scraps of chambray
17 x 13 inches of interlining
18 x 14 inches of backing fabric
Approx. 55 inches of ½-inch-wide velvet ribbon
Embroidery floss and needle
Matching sewing threads

TIPS

- The key to success in making a Log-cabin block is to keep the strips of fabric even in width. An easy way of achieving this is to stick a strip of masking tape on the plate of your sewing machine ¼ inch from the foot and use it as a guide. Alternatively, draw the design on thin paper; stitch along the lines of each strip; and tear off the paper when the block is complete.
- To make a runner for the center of a long table, simply increase the number of blocks.

CONTEMPORARY TWIST
Soft velvet ribbon adds a sophisticated touch to a country-style place mat. Tiny details such as this can transform a traditional design into a contemporary classic.

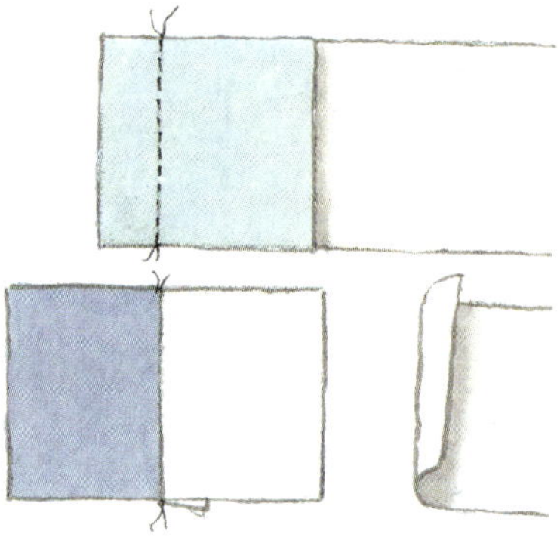

1 Cut the two cream-color linen and floral print pieces for the patchwork into 1-inch-wide strips. Cut six 1-inch squares of chambray. Right sides together and taking a ¼-inch seam, machine-stitch a strip of the linen to one side of a chambray square. Trim the strip level with the edge of the square to make a rectangle, and press the seam toward the linen.

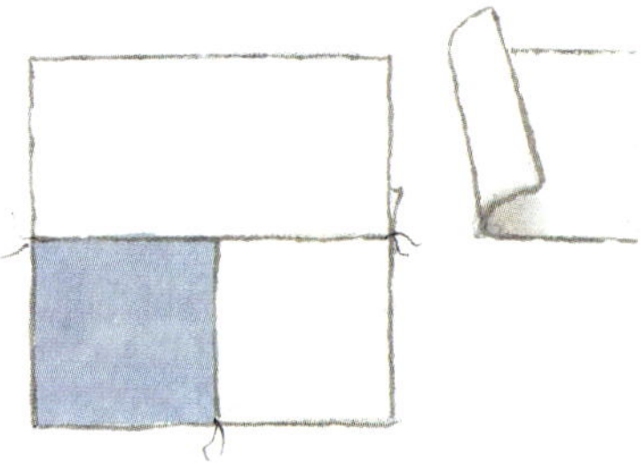

2 Again taking a ¼-inch seam, machine-stitch another strip of linen along one long edge of the rectangle in the same way, and trim it level with the edge to form a square. Press the seam toward the linen.

3 Take a strip of the floral fabric, and taking a ¼-inch seam, machine-stitch it along the other side of the chambray square. Trim and press it as before to make a rectangle. Machine-stitch another strip of the floral fabric to the fourth side of the square to complete the first series of strips.

5 Right sides together, pin two blocks together, placing a linen side of the first block next to a floral side of the next one. Taking a ¼-inch seam, machine-stitch the blocks together, and press open the seam. Join another block to the first two to form a row of three, maintaining the same sequence of dark and pale fabrics. Join the other three blocks together in the same way. Right sides together, machine-stitch the two rows together, placing the pale edge of the second row under the floral edge of the first one. Press open the seam.

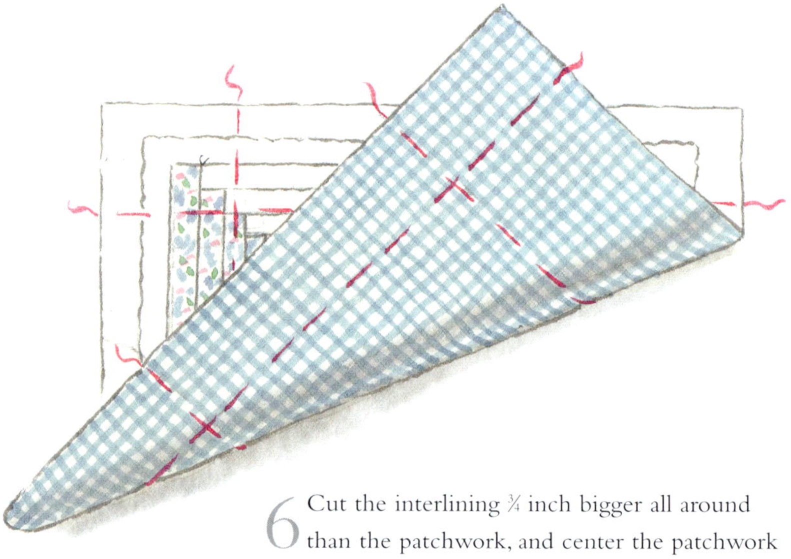

6 Cut the interlining ¾ inch bigger all around than the patchwork, and center the patchwork on top of it, right side up. Cut the backing fabric 1 inch larger all around than the interlining. Place the backing fabric right side down on a flat surface, and center the interlining and patchwork on top of it. Baste the layers together.

4 Continue stitching two strips of each fabric in sequence around the chambray square until sixteen strips in total (eight in each fabric) have been added to form a block; the color placement gives the appearance of a diagonal line across the block, separating light tones from dark tones. Make five more blocks in the same way.

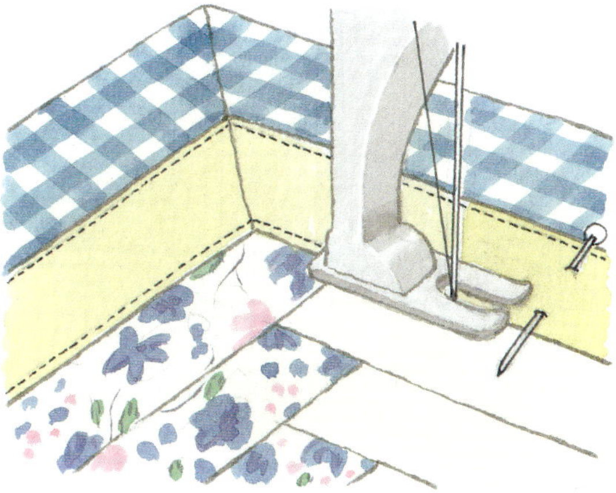

7 Turn the backing fabric over the edges of the interlining to overlap the edges of the patchwork, and pin in place, mitering the corners. (See page 119.) Baste in place. Pin the velvet ribbon to the patchwork to cover the raw edges of the backing fabric, and miter the corners, leaving an even border of backing fabric ¾ inch wide around the outer edge. (See page 119.) Machine-stitch along both sides of the ribbon, stitching close to the edges. Using embroidery floss, tie-quilt the layers together at regular intervals. (See page 118.)

Made from a pale-colored linen for the light areas and a pretty floral print for the dark parts, each square block appears to be divided in half diagonally.

polka-dot tablecloth

Six different fabrics have been chosen for the border of this sumptuous tablecloth. Vintage remnants such as an old floral pillowcase from the 1960s, some striped shirting material, and solid cottons in plum and raspberry, combine to make a vibrant and eclectic design. The border consists of repeated blocks, each one made from different combinations of three fabrics. The dotted fabric used for the tablecloth center is also used for the binding around the border, to provide unity and tie all the patterns together.

The finished tablecloth measures approximately 55 x 47 inches.

YOU WILL NEED

Scraps of fabrics for the patchwork

40 inches of 55-inch-wide fabric for the center of the tablecloth

47 inches of 55-inch-wide fabric for the backing

47 inches of 55-inch-wide cotton interlining

16 inches of 36-inch-wide fabric for the binding

Embroidery floss and needle

CUTTING INSTRUCTIONS

For each block: using the templates on page 123, cut four patches each from templates 1, 2, and 3, using a different fabric for each template.

- Cut one patch from template 4, using the same fabric that you used for template 1.
- Cut enough patches to make 24 blocks in total, using various combinations of fabrics.

TEATIME TREATS
This pretty little cloth, with its polka-dot center and richly colored patchwork border, would brighten up any tea table.

1 Right sides together, pin the longest side of two template 3 triangles to opposite sides of the central template 4 diamond. Taking ¼-inch seams throughout, machine-stitch them together, and press open the seams. Machine-stitch the remaining template 3 triangles to the other sides of the diamond in the same way, and press open the seams. This makes the central square of the block.

2 Machine-stitch one template 2 piece to each side of the central square, and press open the seams. Join one template 1 square to each side of the remaining two template 2 pieces to make two rectangles. Machine-stitch the strips together, matching seams, to complete the block.

4 Lay the backing fabric right side down with the interlining on top. Place the tablecloth top on the interlining, right side up, smoothing all the fabrics out as you go. Working from the center outward, pin safety pins at regular intervals across the tablecloth center, and baste through all layers. Trim the backing and interlining to match the edges of the tablecloth top.

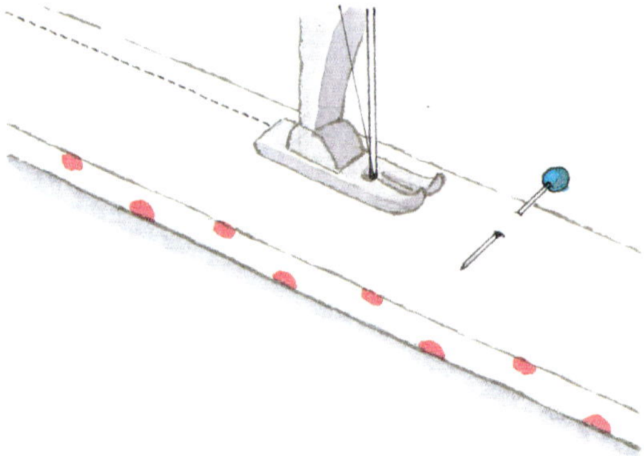

5 Cut strips for the binding 2½ inches wide, and stitch them together so that they will fit along all four edges of the cloth. Press under ½ inch to the wrong side along one long edge of the binding. Right sides together, pin the raw (unturned) edge of the binding strip to the raw edge of the backing, mitering the corners. (See page 119.) Machine-stitch in place, taking a ½-inch seam.

3 Make twenty-three more blocks using your chosen fabric combinations. Taking ¼-inch seams, machine-stitch the blocks together to make two strips of seven blocks and two strips of five blocks. Cut the fabric for the center of the tablecloth to 39½ x 31½ inches. Machine-stitch a five-block strip to each short edge of the center fabric and a seven-block strip to each long edge so that the end blocks match up with those already stitched to the cloth. Press all the seams open.

Each block in the border is made from a different combination of fabrics, so this project is a great way to use up scraps. Always try out different arrangements before you begin stitching to make sure that they work well together.

6 Fold the binding over to the front of the tablecloth so that the folded edge covers the previous line of stitching, and pin it in place. Machine-stitch it in place, stitching close to the folded edge. Using embroidery floss, make evenly spaced ties over the center of the tablecloth to hold the layers together. (See page 118.) Remove any safety pins and basting stitches.

patchwork tablecloth

This country-style tablecloth has an easy look that is just right for a summer tea party but is also smart enough for an informal supper. The cloth is simply constructed from triangles sewn together to make square blocks. It is made predominantly in subtle shades of green, pale blue, shell pink, and cream. The occasional triangle in a bolder floral design adds vibrant highlights and changes the rhythm of what would otherwise be a subdued arrangement. To complete the piece and draw the design elements together, use the same floral fabric to back and bind the cloth.

TIPS

- Choose a mixture of plain and patterned fabrics, and vary the pattern sizes to give your patchwork impact.
- Make sure all of your fabrics can be laundered easily, as tablecloths often become dirty quickly.
- You could use the same techniques to make a set of matching or coordinating napkins or place mats.

The finished tablecloth is approximately 50 inches square.

YOU WILL NEED

Approx. 60 inches of 36-inch-wide fabric in at least four different colors or patterns

50-inch square of white cotton fabric for backing

Four 54 x 2-inch-wide bias-cut strips of one of the patchwork fabrics for the edging

Embroidery floss in a contrasting color

Matching sewing threads

A SPLASH OF SUMMER
This pretty tablecloth is perfect for warm days and evenings in the garden, or you can use it indoors to bring a touch of summer cheer to cooler, darker days.

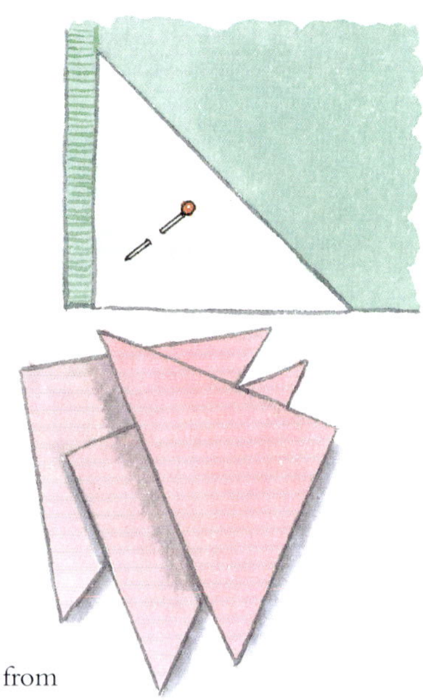

1 Cut fifty 8¼-inch-squares from your chosen fabrics, aligning the fabric on the grain. Then fold one square in half diagonally and cut along the fold to make a template, using this to cut the remaining 99 triangles.

2 Right sides together and taking a ½-inch seam, machine-stitch the triangles together in pairs along one of the short edges to make fifty larger triangles. Then stitch these triangles together in pairs to make twenty five squares.

4 Place the backing fabric right side down on a large flat surface, and place the patchwork right side up on top of it. Working from the center of the piece outward, pin and baste the two layers together. Mark a square grid pattern over the patchwork, working through the center of each patchwork square in both directions. Machine- or hand-quilt, using embroidery floss in a contrasting color.

5 Fold ½ inch of the edging strip under to the wrong side, and press. Right sides together, pin the raw edge of the edging strip to the backing fabric, and stitch around the edges about ½ inch from the edge. Fold the edging over to the front, and pin in place.

3 On a large, flat surface, lay out the squares in five rows of five and move them around until you are happy with the arrangement. Right sides together and taking ½-inch seams, stitch the five squares in each row together. Then stitch the five rows together to make a large square.

6 To complete the tablecloth, machine-stitch the edging, stitching as close to the turned-under edge as possible, or slip-stitch it by hand.

Machine patchwork is ideal for piecing regular, geometric patterns accurately.

picnic blanket

This quilted picnic blanket, with its punchy color combination of lime and jade greens, blue, and pink, is roomy enough for several people to enjoy an outdoor banquet. Generously padded with soft batting, it makes a comfortable cushioned mat that helps to keep damp grass and hard ground from spoiling a relaxing occasion. The overall effect is fresh and vibrant and captures the essence of a perfect summer afternoon. The project would work just as well in the house as a sofa throw or a baby's play mat.

The finished blanket measures 53 inches square.

YOU WILL NEED

Approx. 24 inches of 36-inch-wide fabric in five fabrics for the patchwork

1½ yards of 50-inch-wide lightweight batting

1¾ yards of 60-inch-wide medium-weight canvas for the backing

Embroidery floss

TIP

For extra durability and ease of care, make the backing from waterproof oilcloth or vinyl of the sort used to make "wipeable" tablecloths. It is a little harder to stitch through, but you won't have to worry about grass stains or dampness seeping through from the ground.

PERIOD CHARM
1950s-style prints of plants and flowers help to give this blanket a lovely period feel.

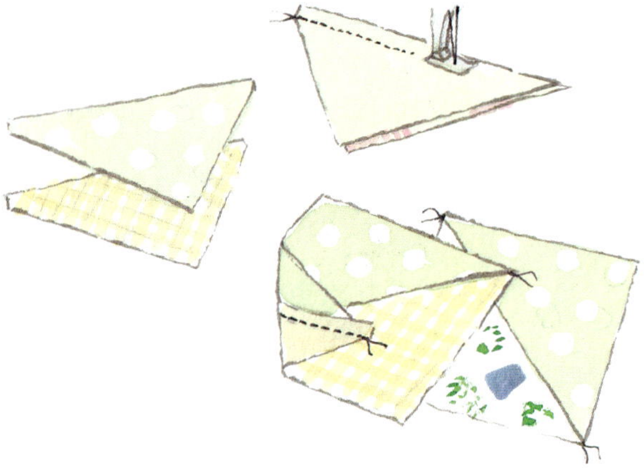

1 Cut out a total of nineteen 11-inch squares from the five patchwork fabrics. Make a pattern for the triangle by drawing an 11-inch square on paper, folding it in half diagonally, and adding a ½-inch seam allowance along the folded edge. Cut out twelve triangles in a selection of the five fabrics.

2 Taking ½-inch seams throughout, machine-stitch the triangles together in pairs along the long edge to make six squares. Trim and press the seams open. There will now be a total of twenty five squares. Lay them out in five rows of five on a flat surface, and move them around until you are happy with the arrangement. Join the squares in rows of five, taking ½-inch seams, and press the seams open. Join the five rows together to make a large square. Trim the seams, and press them open.

4 Place the patchwork right side up onto the wrong side of the canvas to leave approximately 4½ inches of canvas showing all around the edges. Cut across the corner squares on the diagonal from the points where the line of machine-stitched quilting meets the side edges. Baste the patchwork to the canvas. Measure the same border width, and cut away the canvas to correspond to the beveled corner. Turn under and press a ½-inch hem along all edges of the canvas.

3 Lay the patchwork on top of the batting, right side up. Cut the batting to the same size as the patchwork. Working from the center outward, pin and baste the two layers together. Machine-quilt by stitching lines across the middle of each square in both directions.

5 Turn the canvas border to overlap the patchwork by ½ inch, and pin in place, leaving the beveled corners open. Fold over the border along the beveled corners; pleat the fabric so that the edges of the border match; and mark the line where they meet. Turn to the wrong side, and stitch the pleats together along the marked line, leaving the folded hem open to form miters at both corners of the bevel. Trim the seams, and press open. Fold under the hems along the beveled edges, and machine-stitch all around the border close to the edge of the canvas. Tie-quilt all layers together at each intersection between squares using double embroidery floss, cutting the thread ends to ½ inch.

Simple checks and solid colors combine with period prints in a bold display of color and pattern.

CHAPTER 2

Quilts and Throws

Modern heirlooms don't have to take forever to complete, and this chapter contains some exquisite projects that will give you and your family pleasure for years to come. There is a long tradition of using up remnants and leftover scraps of fabric to produce quilts and bed throws, mixing pattern and color in creative ways. Garage-sale and thrift-store finds, mixed with crisp new cottons and lively modern prints, can be chopped up and recycled to create amazing furnishings and accessories. To make your projects even more personal, use fabrics that have strong emotional associations for you: scraps from your baby's first dress, perhaps, or curtains that you had in your first home.

FAMILY QUILT
Using a mix of new and old, pretty florals and cotton prints are matched with linen napkins and embroidery remnants for a fresh, bright look that updates any bedroom.

quilted pillowcase

A quilted pillowcase makes a comfortable padded support when you want to read or have breakfast in bed. This housewife-style pillowcase is embellished with traditional star-shaped patchwork blocks. The pattern is easy to construct because simple triangles and diamonds form each eighth of the block, with two of these pieces stitched together to form a quarter square. Three vintage buttons, with beveled centers that echo the star patchwork pattern, each one a different color, fasten the pillowcase.

The layers of fabric are quilted together by means of a few stitches on every star point, corner, and intersection. These can be done as bartacks on the sewing machine by setting the stitch to zigzag and dropping the feed dog for a few stitches; alternatively, you could work a few satin stitches by hand.

The pillowcase measures 19½ x 29½ inches.

YOU WILL NEED

15 inches of 36-inch-wide patterned fabric for the patchwork stars

24 inches of 36-inch-wide solid-color fabric for the patchwork stars

15 inches of 36-inch-wide fabric for the border

24 inches of 55-inch-wide cotton interlining

24 inches of 55-inch-wide fabric for the backing

24 inches of 55-inch-wide fabric for the pillowcase back

Three buttons

CUTTING INSTRUCTIONS

- *For the patchwork:* using the templates on page 122, cut 48 patches from template 1 in patterned fabric, 48 pieces from template 2 in solid-colored fabric, and 48 pieces from template 3 in solid-colored fabric.
- *For the borders:* cut two strips measuring 24½ x 3 inches, one strip measuring 20½ x 3 inches, and one strip measuring 20½ x 5 inches.
- *For the backing:* cut a piece of fabric measuring 20½ x 30 inches.
- *For the pillowcase back:* cut a piece of fabric 20½ x 36½ inches.

PATTERN POWER
The stars in this pillowcase are pieced from a small-patterned print—far more effective than a solid color, which can look somewhat flat and uninteresting.

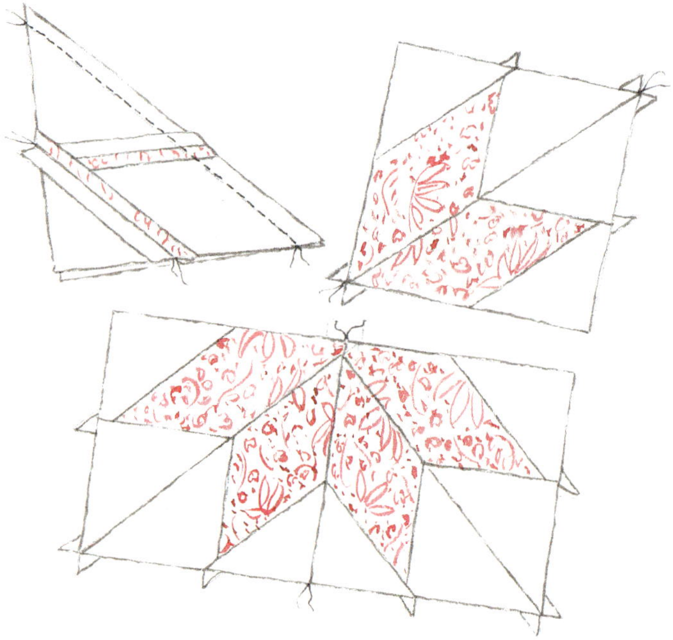

1 Right sides together, pin a triangle from template 2 to one side of a template 1 diamond, and machine-stitch, taking a ¼-inch seam. Press the seam open. Pin a triangle from template 3 to the opposite side of the same diamond; machine-stitch; and press as before. Make up seven more patches in the same way.

2 Right sides together, pin two patches together, matching the edges of the diamonds and the template 3 triangle patches. Machine-stitch, taking a ¼-inch seam, and press open the seam. This completes one-quarter of the star. Make up the remaining three-quarters in the same way. Right sides together, pin and machine-stitch two quarters together, matching the diamonds and the template 2 triangle patches, and press open the seam. Complete the other half of the star in the same way. Join the two halves across the center to complete the star. Make five more stars.

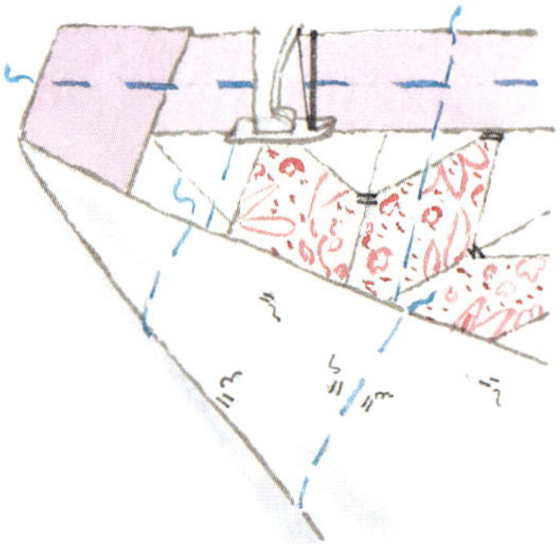

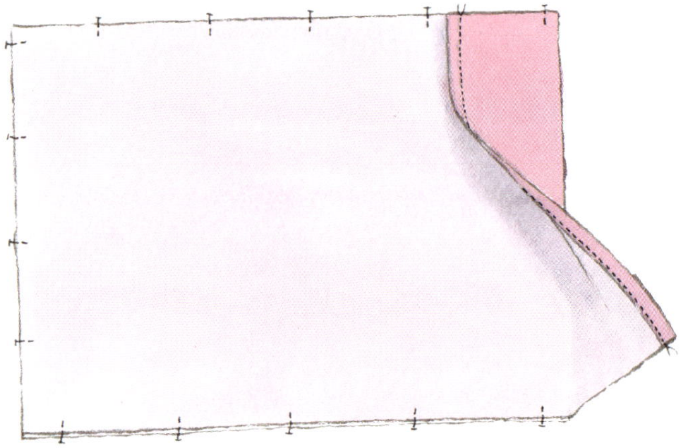

5 Cut the interlining to the same size as the patchwork. Wrong sides together, baste the patchwork to the interlining. Right sides together, pin the backing fabric along the opening edge of the pillowcase, and machine-stitch, taking a ½-inch seam. Turn to the right side, and baste the backing to the back of the interlining through all layers. With the feed dog lowered and the stitch set to zigzag, work small bartacks at every star point, center, and intersection to quilt and hold the layers together; alternatively, work a few satin stitches by hand.

6 Turn under ¼ inch and then ½ inch along one short edge of the pillowcase back, and machine-stitch. Right sides together, pin the back to the pillowcase front so that the hemmed edge extends 6 inches beyond the pillowcase. Fold the extended area back to make the inside flap. Stitch down both long sides and the pinned short edge. Neaten the seam with a zigzag stitch.

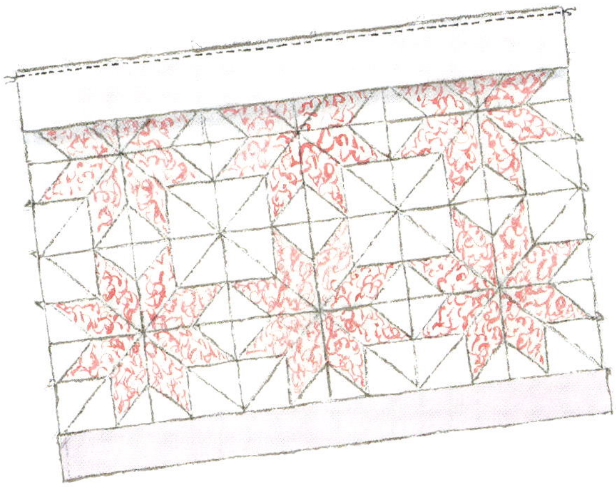

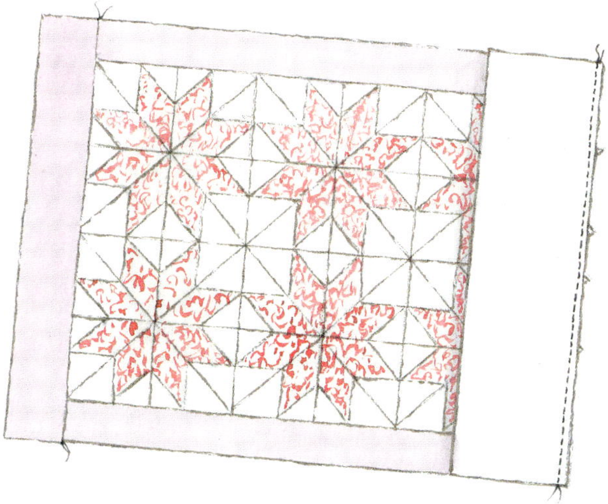

3 Join the six stars together in two rows of three, to make a rectangle. Right sides together, pin and then machine-stitch one of the long strips of border fabric to one long edge of the patchwork rectangle, taking a ½-inch seam. Press open the seam. Pin and then machine-stitch the other long strip of border fabric to the other long edge of the patchwork, and press open the seam.

4 Right sides together, pin the narrow strip of border fabric to the left-hand short edge of the patchwork. Machine-stitch, taking a ½-inch seam, and press open the seam. Right sides together, stitch the remaining piece of border fabric to the other short edge of the patchwork. (This will be the opening end of the pillowcase.)

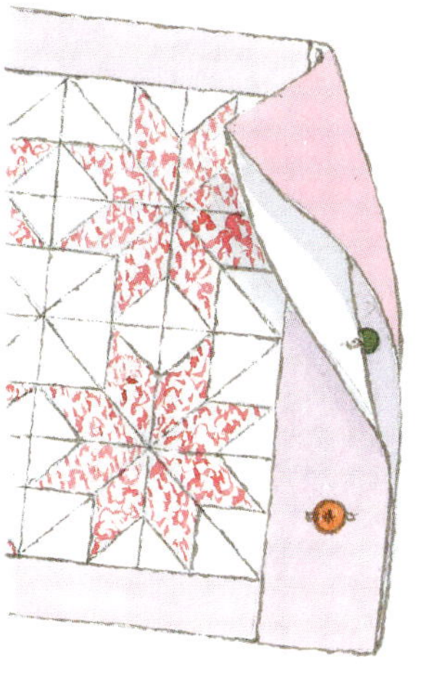

7 Turn the pillowcase right side out, and press the seams. Remove any basting stitches. Make three evenly spaced buttonholes along the opening-edge border, and stitch the buttons onto the flap beneath. (See page 119.)

The star-cut pattern inside these buttons echoes the patchwork motif. Thrift stores are often a good source of inexpensive, interesting buttons.

floral bolster cover

Bolster pillows provide extra comfort in a chair or sofa with no arms, as well as adding interesting shapes when mixed in among rectangular and square pillows. A tube with circular ends is a versatile pillow shape that gives comfortable support, molding itself into the small of your back.

The patchwork bands that decorate this pillow are made from squares, with one color repeatedly zigzagging through to unify the pattern. A zipper stitched along the back makes it easy to remove the cover for laundering when necessary. Decorative trims in a color that complements the patchwork fabrics provide a pretty finishing touch; however, the bolster would look just as good without trimming.

The bolster cover is 17½ inches long and 6¾ inches in diameter.

YOU WILL NEED

Scraps of fabric for the patchwork
28 inches of 55-inch-wide fabric
20 inches of 55-inch-wide cotton interlining
20 inches of 55-inch-wide backing fabric
12-inch zipper
Approx. 8 feet of crochet lace (optional)
Bolster cushion pad
Matching sewing threads

MODERN TONES
Neutral brown-and-cream abstract florals, with hints of soft yellows and pinks, make a harmonious color scheme.

TIP

Although patchwork is a great way to use up tiny scraps of fabric, you still need to plan your color scheme. Here, yellow squares predominate and hold the whole design together.

1 Cut twenty-six 2½-inch squares from a solid-colored fabric (I used yellow), and twenty-six 2½-inch squares from an assortment of patchwork fabrics. Arrange the squares to make four lines of thirteen squares each, alternating the solid-colored squares with the assorted squares. Right sides together and taking ¼-inch seams, machine-stitch the squares together to make four strips, and press the seams open. Machine-stitch the strips together in pairs, again taking ¼-inch seams, to complete the two patchwork bands. Press open the seams.

2 From the main fabric, cut a center panel measuring 5 x 24½ inches, two side panels measuring 3½ x 24½ inches, and two circles 6¾ inches in diameter. Right sides together, machine-stitch one patchwork band to each long edge of the center panel, taking a ¼-inch seam. Trim the patchwork bands to the same length. Machine-stitch one side panel to the other edge of each patchwork band, again taking a ¼-inch seam. This completes the bolster top.

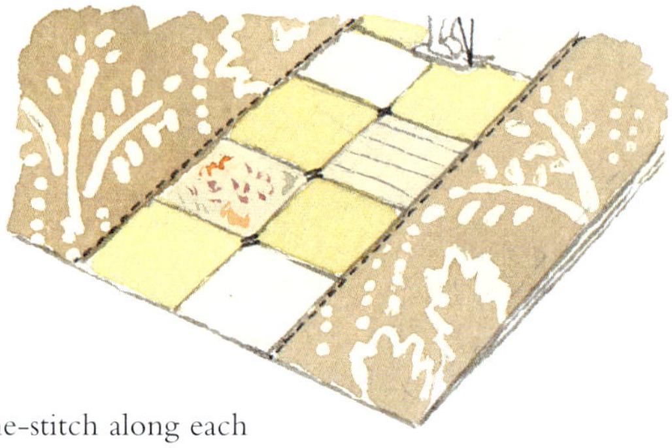

4 Machine-stitch along each edge of each patchwork band to quilt the layers together. Sew bartacks along the center of each patchwork band, at the points where two squares meet, by setting the stitch to the widest zigzag setting and dropping the feed dog underneath the machine foot. Machine-stitch a guide line along each long edge of the bolster top, ⅜ inch in from the edge, stitching through all layers.

5 Bring the short ends of the bolster together, and slip-stitch together for 3¼ inches at both ends, leaving a 12-inch opening in the middle. Pin the zipper into the opening, and machine-stitch it in place, using a zipper foot. With the zipper open, turn the bolster wrong side out.

3 Cut the interlining and backing fabric to the same size as the bolster top. Place the bolster top right side up on top of the interlining and the backing fabric right side down on top of the bolster top. Pin and machine-stitch along both short edges, taking ½-inch seams. Press the seams flat. Turn to the right side so that the interlining is sandwiched between the bolster top and the backing fabric, and pin the raw, long edges together.

Vintage crochet edgings in different widths can be stitched onto the completed pillow as an extra decorative feature.

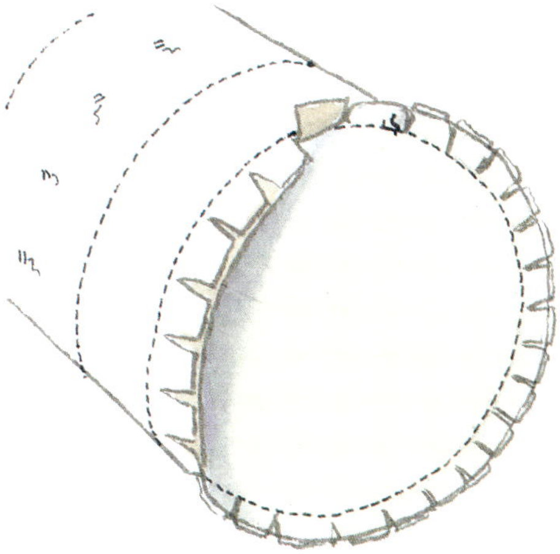

6 Right sides together, pin a circle piece into each bolster end, clipping up to the guide line where necessary to follow the curves, and machine-stitch in place, taking a ½-inch seam. Turn right side out, and insert the bolster pad. For an extra decorative touch, pin crochet lace along the edges of the patchwork bands, and slip-stitch it in place.

crib quilt

The hand-embroidered panels in this charming little crib quilt are made from recycled table scarves and antimacassars: each panel tells a story. These lovingly worked embroidered items can be found at craft fairs and garage sales and are often made from good-quality linen. It is very satisfying to give them a more permanent use. As for the decorative finishing touches, a floral tablecloth has been used to make the most of the border and sashing strips, while rickrack braid sewn around each panel adds a decorative touch to the overall design and serves the useful purpose of holding all the layers together.

The finished quilt measures approximately 36 x 48 inches.

YOU WILL NEED

2¼ yards of 44-inch-wide gingham

1¼ yards of 55-inch-wide 2 oz cotton batting

12 pieces of embroidered fabric 7 inches square for the feature panels

24 inches of 36-inch-wide fabric for the edging

Scraps of six fabrics for the sashing strips and posts

8½ yards of rickrack braid

Matching sewing threads

CUTTING INSTRUCTIONS

Draw and cut paper patterns to the following sizes:

- *Pattern A*: 10½ x 3¼ inches
- *Pattern B*: 3¼ x 3¼ inches
- *Pattern C*: 10½ x 2 inches
- *Pattern D*: 2 x 2 inches
- *Pattern E*: 2 x 3¼ inches

Cut the following number of fabric patches from each pattern:

- *Pattern A*: cut eight from edging fabric and nine from the patchwork fabric selection.
- *Pattern B*: cut six from the patchwork fabric selection.
- *Pattern C*: cut fourteen from edging fabric.
- *Pattern D*: cut four from the patchwork fabric selection.
- *Pattern E*: cut ten from the patchwork fabric selection.

SAFETY INFORMATION

Crib quilts are not suitable for use for infants under 12 months old.

1 Cut a 37 x 49-inch piece of gingham and twelve 10½-inch gingham squares. Cut a piece of batting the same size as the large piece of gingham backing fabric. Lay the batting on the wrong side of the backing. Baste them together at regular intervals.

2 Turn under ½-inch hems along all four edges of each of the embroidered panels. Pin, then baste each one to the center of a gingham square. Machine-stitch in place, stitching close to the edges.

5 Join the strips together to make the quilt front, sewing an outside-edge strip along the left-hand edge of one panel strip, matching seams where the strips meet. Sew a narrow center strip to the other side of the panel strip; then continue joining the strips together, ending with the other outside-edge strip.

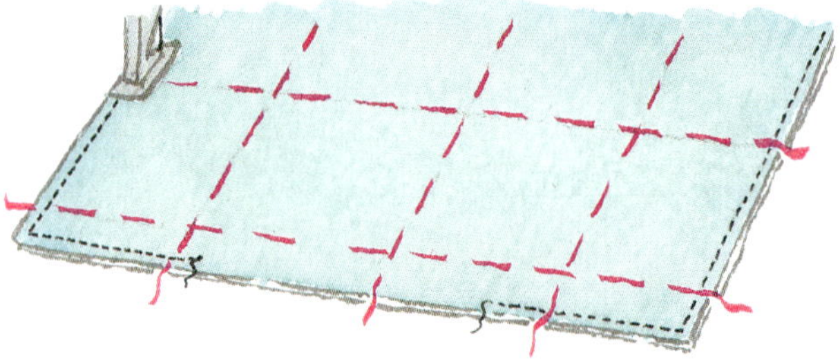

6 Right sides together, pin the quilt front to the backing and batting. Machine-stitch along all sides to form a bag, taking a ½-inch seam and leaving an opening of about 6 inches along one edge. Turn the bag right side out; press the edges; and slip-stitch the opening closed. Lay the quilt flat; then working from the center outward, pin and baste the layers together.

3 Join panels in vertical rows as follows: Right sides together, pin one C patch along the top edge of one gingham panel square, and machine-stitch, taking a ½-inch seam, then press the seam flat. Sew one A patch along the bottom edge of the same panel square. Add two more panels in the same way, separating them with A patches, and complete the strip by adding a C patch along the bottom edge. Make two more strips in the same way.

4 Now make the two narrow center strips that run between the vertical rows, machine-stitching the pieces together in the following sequence: E, A, B, A, B, A, B, A, E. For the two outside-edge strips, stitch the pieces in the following sequence: D, C, E, C, E, C, E, C, D.

7 Pin rickrack braid around each of the feature squares, and machine-stitch it in place, stitching through all the layers to hold them together.

A small gingham check and strips of sashing made from reused fabric set off the simply embroidered panels to perfection.

bed throw

It's fascinating to see how many variations there are on patchwork block patterns. This charming bed throw is based on a traditional pattern known as Jacob's Ladder. When you use different tones of similar colors in an ordered way, you create diagonal stripes that add movement and rhythm to the design. Patterned fabrics combine with solid block colors in light, medium, and dark tones of lavender and cream, creating a clean and fresh-looking combination; a wide linen border provides a generous and luxurious finish. Machine-stitched bartacks at every seam intersection are a quick and effective method of quilting the fabrics together.

The finished throw measures approximately 50 x 40 inches.

YOU WILL NEED

16 inches of 55-inch-wide cotton fabric in a dark tone
Scraps of cotton fabrics in light and medium tones
44 inches of 55-inch-wide cotton fabric for the backing
44 inches of 55-inch-wide batting
40 inches of 55-inch-wide linen for the border

TONAL CONTRASTS
As in so many traditional patchwork block designs, the contrast between light, medium, and dark tones of the same color is critical in establishing the overall pattern.

TIP

A speedy way of cutting fabrics for a pattern that is based around squares and triangles is to use a rotary cutter. (See page 115.)

1 For each block, using the templates on page 126, cut five squares from medium-toned fabric and four triangles each from light- and dark-toned fabrics. Machine-stitch the light and dark triangles together in pairs along their long edges to make squares, taking ¼-inch seams. Press open the seams.

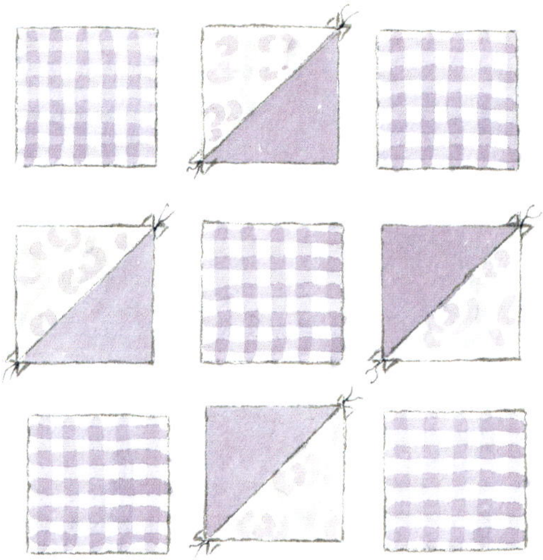

2 Lay out the solid squares and pieced squares in three rows of three, alternating them as shown. Note that, to create the effect of a light diagonal line running through the quilt, the light triangles must form the top of the square in patches 2 and 4, and the bottom of the square in patches 6 and 8.

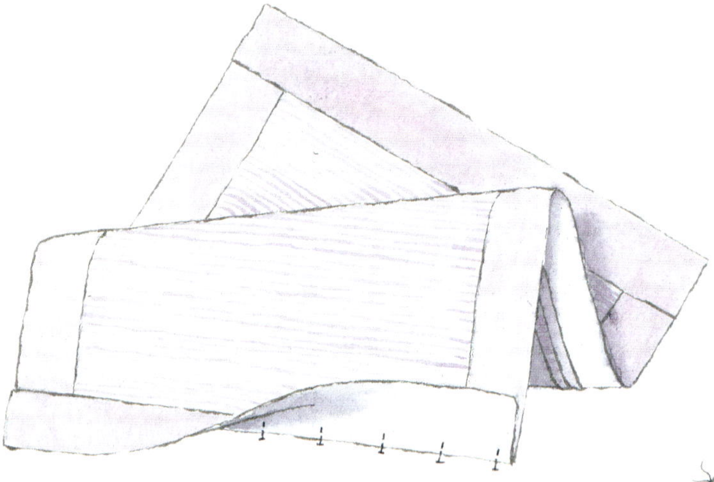

5 Cut a piece of backing fabric the same size as the patchwork. Cut four strips of border fabric 4½ x 45 inches for the side borders, and four strips 4½ x 40 inches for the top and bottom borders. Right sides together, pin and machine-stitch one border strip along each long edge of the backing fabric, taking a ¼-inch seam. Press open the seams, and trim the border fabric so that the ends are level with the backing. Stitch the top and bottom borders to the two short sides of the backing fabric and across the ends of the side borders in the same way. Add border strips to the patchwork top in the same way.

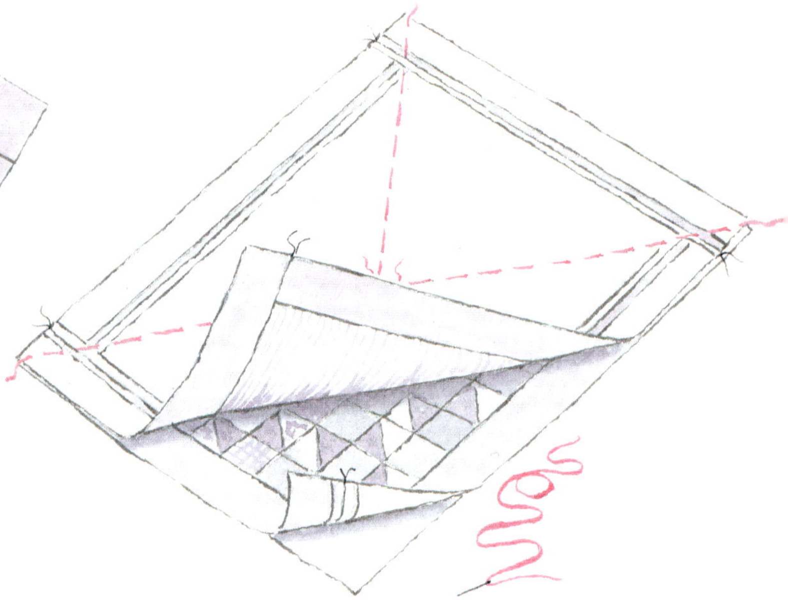

6 Place the patchwork right side up on top of the batting, with the backing right side down on top of the patchwork. Working from the center outward, pin or baste the layers together. Machine-stitch around the edges, taking a ½-inch seam and leave a gap of about 6 inches in one side. Trim the seams. Turn the quilt right side out so that the batting is sandwiched in between the backing and quilt top, and slip-stitch the gap closed.

3 Right sides together and taking a ¼-inch seam, stitch the patches together in three rows of three. Press open the seams. Now stitch the three rows together in the same way, again taking ¼-inch seams, and taking care to align the seams. Make 11 more nine-patch blocks in the same way.

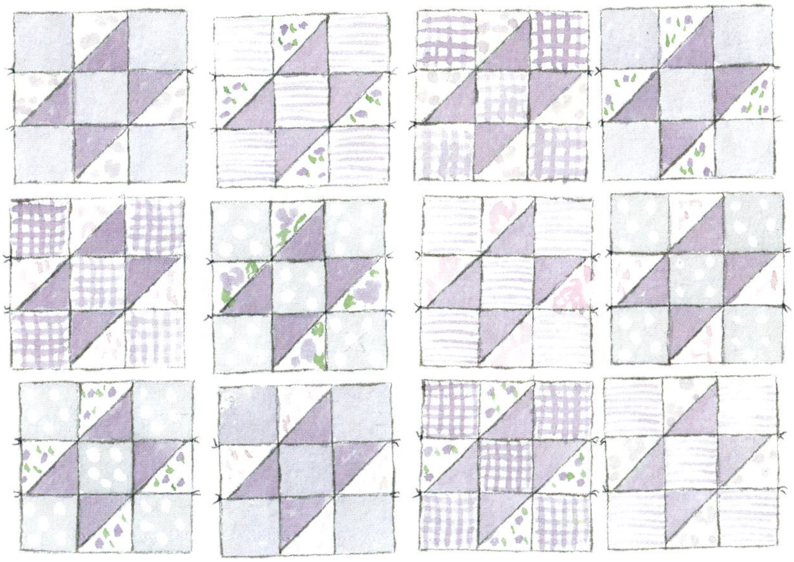

4 Lay out the blocks in three rows of four, making sure you maintain the same orientation so that you do not lose the effect of the diagonal lines. Machine-stitch four blocks together to make each row, taking ¼-inch seams, and press open the seams. Then machine-stitch the three rows together, again taking ¼-inch seams, and press open the seams.

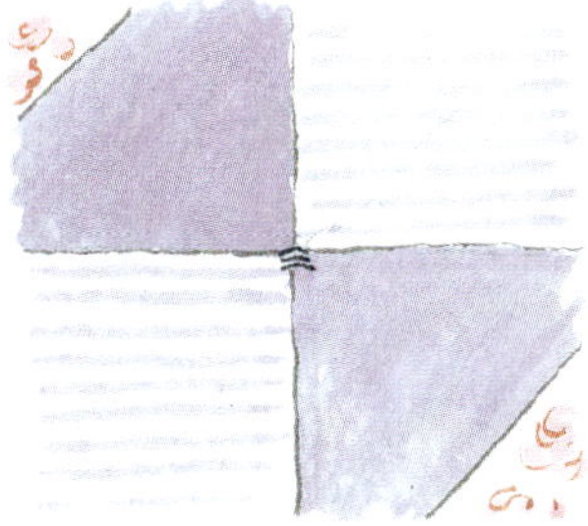

7 To quilt the layers together, topstitch along the inside edge of the border, and sew bartacks at the junctions of the squares, by setting the stitch to the widest zigzag setting and dropping the feed dog underneath the machine foot. (See page 117.)

Because this throw is assembled using the "bagging" technique (page 117), there is no need to add a separate binding. The wide linen border finishes the bed throw neatly but does not overpower it.

square-patterned quilt

This cheerful square-patterned quilt is surprisingly easy to make. As it is constructed row by row, it can easily be adapted to fit a larger-sized bed by adding extra rows of squares until it is the size you want. Once you have decided on the position of the squares, simply sew them into strips, and stitch the strips directly onto the batting and backing fabrics to form pockets. At this point, you can pop squares of batting or wool fleece into the pockets to give more padding and insulation if required.

Here the brightly colored squares are set out in a symmetrical way, but you could arrange them randomly if you prefer, which would be a good way of using up smaller scraps. With pink as the general color theme, the fabrics range from solid colors to florals and stripes, with occasional flashes of brighter shades to provide a change of pace. Small buttons and felt rosettes used on traditional mattresses (available from upholstery suppliers) are used to decorate some of the squares.

The finished quilt is approximately 50 inches square.

YOU WILL NEED

Forty-nine 8-inch squares of fabric for the patchwork (Here ten different fabrics are used, positioned symmetrically, but you could use completely random patterns if you prefer)

51 inches of 55-inch-wide fabric for the backing

51 inches of 55-inch-wide cotton batting

16 inches of 36-inch-wide fabric for the edging

Felt washers and small buttons (optional)

Matching sewing threads

DECORATIVE AND FUNCTIONAL
Decorative buttons are a quick-and-easy way of holding the three layers of a quilt together.

1 Lay all the squares out on a large, flat surface in seven rows of seven, and move them around until you're happy with the arrangement. Right sides together and taking a ½-inch seam, machine-stitch the first two squares of the first row together. Press the seam open, then join the other five squares from that row in the same way to form a long strip. Make six more rows in the same way, to give a total of seven strips.

2 Lay the backing fabric right side down, and place the batting on top of it. Pin and then baste the two layers together. Place the first strip of squares right side up along one edge of the batting, and pin it in place. Machine-stitch along both short edges and the long outside edge of the strip ½ inch in from the edges. Machine-stitch down each seam between the squares to form seven pockets that are open along one edge. You can add extra padding in each pocket at this point if you wish.

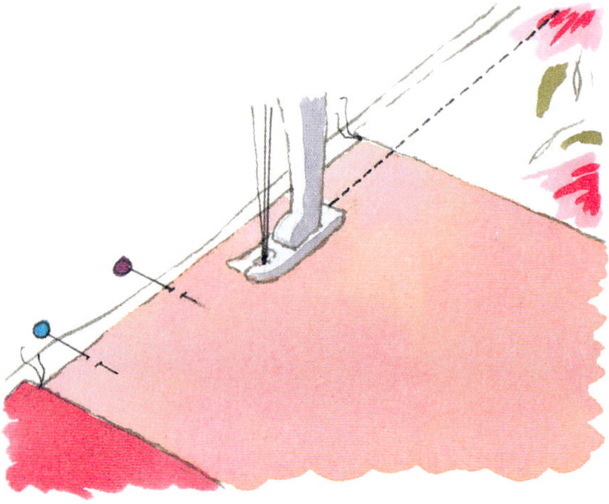

4 Continue to construct the quilt strip by strip, making rows of pockets before sewing on the next strip. When you have sewn the last strip, machine-stitch along the top edge to close the pockets. Trim away any excess backing fabric and batting to match the sides of the quilt top.

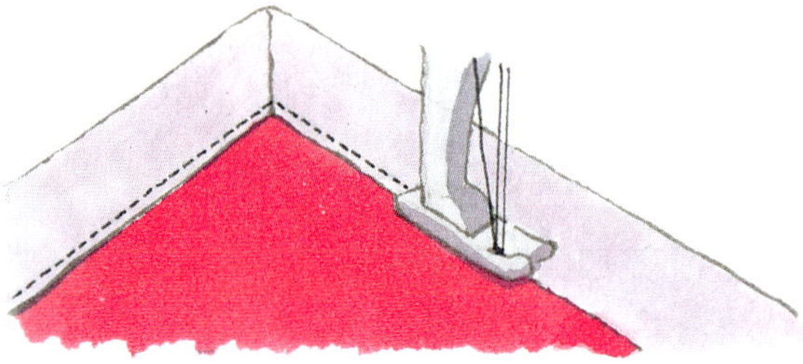

5 Cut strips of edging fabric 2½ inches wide, and join them together to make one continuous strip long enough to go along the four sides of the quilt. Press under ½ inch to the wrong side along one edge of the binding. With the right side of the unturned edge of the binding facing the wrong side of the quilt, pin and then machine-stitch the binding around the edges of the quilt, mitering the corners and taking a ½-inch seam. Fold the binding over to the right side so that the turned edge overlaps the stitched line ½ inch in from the quilt's edges. Pin and then machine-stitch in place close to the folded edge. Press the edging flat.

3 Right sides together, pin the second strip right side down along the unstitched edge of the first strip, and machine-stitch, taking a ½-inch seam, thus closing the first row of pockets. Fold the second strip over to the right side; press; and pin to the batting and backing fabrics. Machine-stitch down each side edge and along each seam between the squares as before to make the second row of seven pockets.

6 Make decorative rosettes using felt washers and buttons if required, and stitch to the center of some of the squares, stitching through all layers.

The striped backing fabric used here is so pretty that you could even display the reverse side of the quilt.

family quilt

This generously sized, cozy quilt is a great one in which to snuggle. It is also surprisingly easy and quick to make. Panels made up of patchwork rectangles are arranged in a regular formation on the layers of backing fabric and batting, and a fabric grid is then sewn on top to secure them in place. Chambray rosettes made from the same fabric as the border are also used in a regular arrangement, quilting the layers of fabric together and providing an extra decorative detail.

The finished quilt measures approximately 68 x 78 inches.

YOU WILL NEED

Approx. 16 inches each of six 55-inch-wide fabrics for the patchwork (or smaller amounts of more fabrics)

2 yards of 90-inch-wide batting

4 yards of 36-inch-wide fabric for the backing

4 yards of 55-inch-wide fabric for the bands and border

Matching sewing threads

CUTTING INSTRUCTIONS

Following the diagram on page 60, cut out pieces from the assorted patchwork fabrics to make up the panels as follows:

- Four corner panels, each made up of four 6¾ x 7¾-inch rectangles
- Two center edge panels, each made up of five 8¾ x 7¾-inch rectangles and two 8¾ x 4⅜-inch rectangles
- One center panel made up of six 8¾ x 10¾-inch rectangles, two 8¾-inch squares, and one 8¾ x 14⅝-inch rectangle
- Two side panels, each made up of three 12½ x 10¾-inch rectangles

FLOWER POWER
Solid blues combine with pretty floral prints and scraps of antique embroidery in this charming country-style quilt.

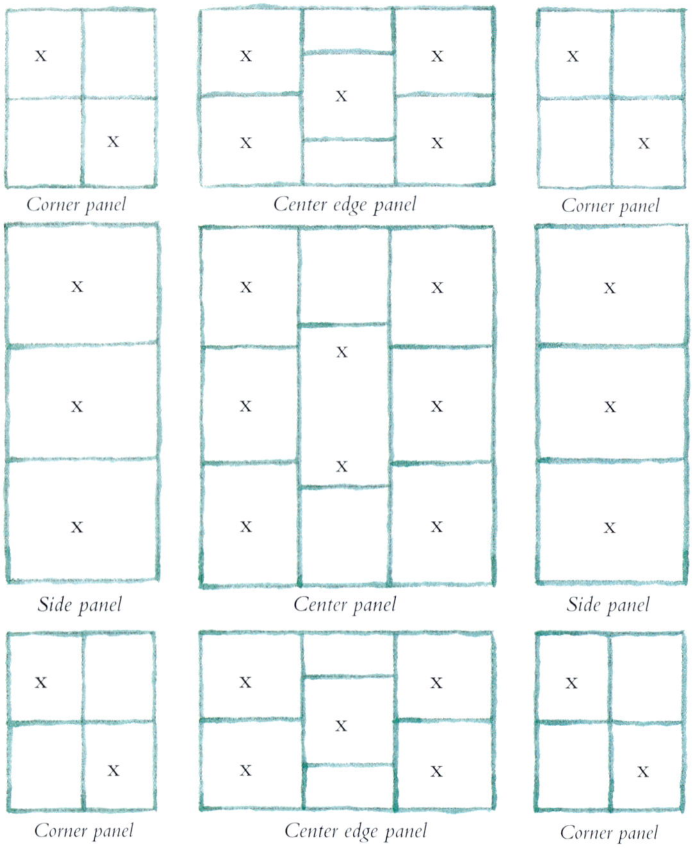

"X" marks the position of the rosettes that are stitched on in step 7.

1 Right sides together and taking ½-inch seams, machine-stitch the pieces for the panels together, as shown, pressing the seams open as you go. Make four corner panels, two center edge panels, one center panel, and two side panels.

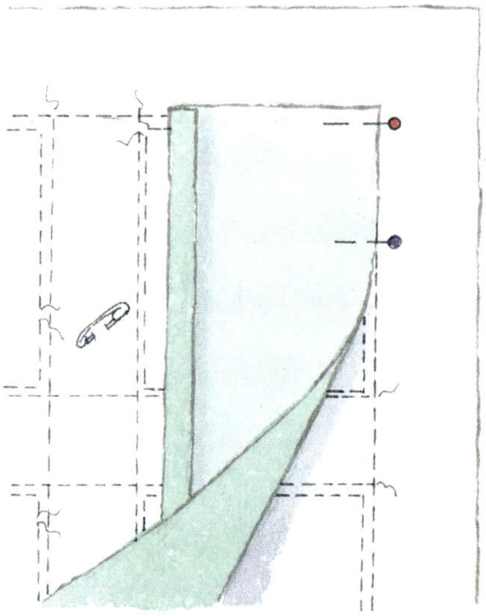

4 From the border fabric, cut four 6½ x 68½-inch strips. Press under ½ inch along both long edges of all four strips. Place two strips right sides up across the quilt between the panels so that the strip edges overlap the panels by ½ inch; pin; and topstitch in place, cutting ends level with the panel edges. Place the remaining two strips between the panels running down the quilt in the same way, and topstitch in place.

5 From the border fabric, cut two 12 x 70-inch strips. Turn under ½ inch to the wrong side along one long edge of each strip, and press. Right sides together, pin one strip against the side edge of the quilt backing so that the strip's raw edge follows the guide line stitched in step 2. Stitch in place, taking a ½-inch seam. Fold the strip over to the right side of the quilt so that the folded edge aligns with the line of stitching. Topstitch close to the fold. Attach the other strip to the other side of the quilt in the same way.

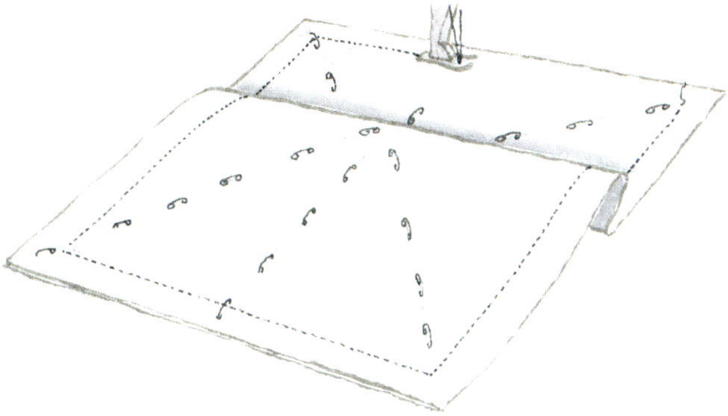

2 Cut the backing fabric in half lengthwise, and join the two pieces to make a piece measuring 72 x 110 inches, big enough to back the quilt. Lay the backing fabric right side down with the batting on top, and cut both layers to 68 inches wide x 78 inches long. Working from the center outward and smoothing the fabrics as you go, pin the layers together. Machine-stitch a guide line around all four sides, 5 inches in from the edges.

3 Pin the panels on top of the batting and backing, following the diagram, so that the outside panel edges are parallel with the edges of the batting and 5 inches in from the edges and the center panels have 4¼-inch gaps between them. Safety-pin each panel to the batting and backing, and baste them in place. Machine-stitch along the seam lines to quilt the layers together.

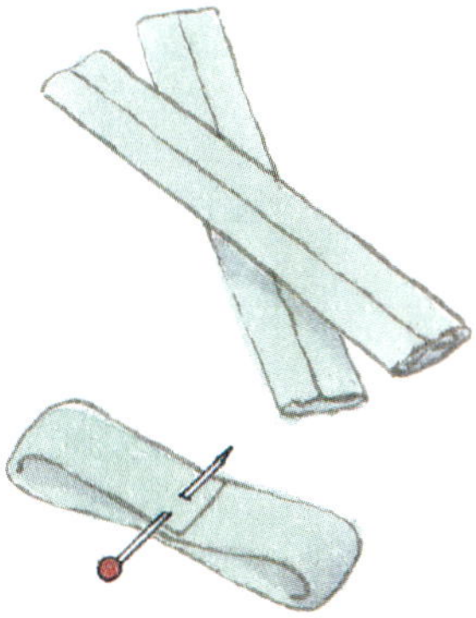

6 From the border fabric, cut two 12 x 69½-inch strips. Turn under ½ inch to the wrong side along one long edge of each strip, and press. Right sides together, pin the top border to the back of the quilt, along the top edge, so that the strip's raw edge follows the guide line stitched in step 2 and ½ inch extends beyond the edge of the quilt on each side. Fold the ½-inch overlap to the right side down both side edges. Fold the strip over to the right side of the quilt, as in step 5, and topstitch close to the fold. Slip-stitch the ends of the border closed. Attach the other strip to the bottom edge of the quilt in the same way.

7 To make the rosettes, cut long strips from leftover border fabric 1½ inches wide. Fold a strip in half lengthwise, right sides together, and stitch along the long raw edge to make a tube. Turn the tube right side out, with the seam running down the center of one side, and press. Cut into 3-inch lengths. With the seam facing upward, fold the ends into the center, overlapping them by ¼ inch. Pin the two ends together in the center. Place a rosette in each position, as shown in the diagram, and machine-stitch across the center of each rosette, stitching through all layers. You will need 32 rosettes.

Simple little fabric rosettes adorn the quilt at regular intervals.

CHAPTER 3

Curtains and Cushions

Even the most stylish of furniture needs a helping hand every now and then, and this chapter includes several imaginative ideas for patchworked and quilted chair cushions. Windows, too—often the focal point of a room—can be given a quick-and-easy makeover with simply pieced but elegant curtains.

CHILD'S SEAT CUSHION
Created from worn children's clothes and junior castoffs, this chair cushion transforms a battered piece of furniture into a country-style adornment for the nursery.

dining-chair cushion

A set of classic dining chairs will look even more elegant with matching cushions, while the extra padding makes the seats more comfortable for a lengthy dinner party. You could make other covers for different occasions—or even use another color of linen for each cover, with a slightly varied patchwork block on each chair back. Washable covers protect your chairs and are practical, too. Remember to launder all of the fabrics before you begin so that you know they will not shrink or fade, and will remain in good condition.

The chair cover fits an upholstered dining chair 38 (H) x 21 (W) x 20 (D) inches. Adjust it to fit your own chair.

YOU WILL NEED

Scraps of five different fabrics for the patchwork
Pattern paper
36 inches of 55-inch-wide linen for the main fabric
Approx. 13 feet of ribbon for the ties
72 inches of 55-inch-wide backing fabric
72 inches of 55-inch-wide cotton interlining
20 inches of 36-inch-wide fabric for the edging
Matching sewing threads

RESTRAINED ELEGANCE
The majority of this cover is made from neutral creams and taupes, with patterned fabrics only in the patchwork star on the chair back—a refined combination for formal dining.

CUTTING INSTRUCTIONS

Using the templates on page 126—127, make paper patterns. From the selection of patchwork fabrics, cut three pattern 1 pieces in each of two fabrics, six pairs of pattern 2 pieces, 2 pairs of pattern 3 pieces, four pattern 4 pieces, two pattern 5 pieces, and two pattern 6 pieces.

child's seat cushion

Adding a lively seat cushion to a child's chair that has seen better days is a great way of dressing it up. A pretty frilled skirt softens the lines all the way around. You can make the cushion using scraps of cotton prints mixed with pieces of chambray, ticking, and solid-color fabrics. Clothes that your children have outgrown are a good source of fabrics, as they are often made from prints in simple designs that work well in a nursery or a child's bedroom. Machine-stitching adds the strength that soft furnishings need to withstand use by children. Cut all of the squares to make the seat, and lay them on the floor before you begin sewing, rearranging them until the positions look right.

The seat cushion is approximately 12 inches square. Adjust the size of the squares to fit your own chair if necessary.

YOU WILL NEED

Scraps of at least seven different fabrics for the seat cushion and skirt, some patterned and some solid colors

12-inch square of lightweight batting

16 inches of 36-inch-wide fabric for backing

Pattern paper

1 yard of 1-inch-wide ribbon for the ties

TIPS

- Although the placement of the squares is random, aim for a good balance of solid colors and patterned fabrics.
- As with all patchwork, when you're mixing lots of fabrics together, it's a good idea to choose ones that are of a similar weight.

SIMPLE SQUARES
This pretty seat cushion, pieced from soft-colored squares, would make a lovely addition to any little girl's bedroom.

1 Cut out twenty-five 3½-inch squares from the selection of fabrics. Lay them out in five rows of five squares so that the squares contrast in color and pattern, and move them around to form a satisfactory arrangement. Right sides together and taking ½-inch seams, machine-stitch five squares together to make a row. Make five rows, and then join these rows together to make a large square. Trim the seam allowances, and press open the seams as you go.

2 Cut a piece of batting and a piece of fabric for the backing the same size as the patchwork panel. Place the backing fabric right side down on your work surface, with the batting on top of it and the patchwork panel right side up on top of the batting. Working from the center outward, pin and baste all three layers together.

4 To make the skirt, cut eighteen rectangles of different fabrics measuring 5 x 4½ inches. Pin and machine-stitch thirteen pieces together to make a long strip, joining them along the short edges and taking ½-inch seams. Pin and machine-stitch the remaining five pieces in the same way to make a second strip for the skirt back. On the first strip, turn under a hem of ¼ inch followed by ½ inch down both short edges and one long edge. Pin; press; and machine-stitch. Hem the second strip in the same way.

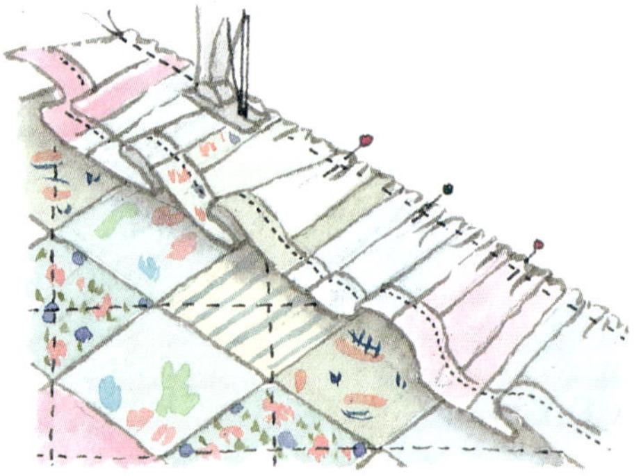

5 Make a paper pattern by placing a piece of paper on the chair seat and drawing a line around the chair's edge and the upright posts on the chair back. Add a ½-inch seam allowance all around, and cut it out. Place the pattern centrally on the patchwork; pin it to the material; and cut the fabric to shape. Turn under ½-inch hems on the cover along the cutout sections at each side of the chair back. Gather the skirt strips along the raw edges so that the long strip fits around the sides and front of the seat cover and the short strip fits along the back of the seat. Right sides together, pin the strips in place on the seat cover, arranging the gathers evenly, and machine-stitch in place. Press open the seams.

3 Machine-stitch lines running diagonally across the seat cover in both directions, starting from the outer corners of the seat cover and from the outer corners of the middle squares on each side. Remove the pins and basting stitches.

6 Cut the ribbon for the ties into four equal lengths, and pin them in position on the back of the skirt so that you can tie them around the back of the chair. Machine-stitch the ties in place.

The diagonal lines of quilting add an interesting contrast of texture to the simple design of patchwork squares.

kitchen-chair cushion

Neat and practical, a tailored cushion will soften the wooden seat of any painted kitchen chair. This clean and bright color combination uses scraps of 1950s-style fabrics and junk-shop finds to make bands of interlocking triangles, which alternate with strips of crisp pink-and-white ticking. Piping made from the same ticking fabric gives the cushion a professional-looking finish.

The finished cushion measures approximately 15¾ x 17¾ inches.

YOU WILL NEED

20-inch square of 1-inch-thick foam for the cushion pad

Pattern paper

A selection of cotton fabric scraps for the patchwork

24 x 20 inches of ticking

20-inch square of interlining

20-inch square of calico

20-inch square of patterned fabric for the seat cushion back

12 x 20 inches of patterned fabric for the ties

Fabric cut on the bias and 1½ yards of piping cord to make the piping or 1½ yards of ready-made piping

Matching sewing threads and soft embroidery floss and needle

10-inch zipper

BUDGET BRIGHTENER

Making a patterned seat cushion is a great way to add color to a room at very little expense.

TIPS

- A zipper in the top of the cushion makes it easy to remove it for laundering.
- Don't skimp on the fabric for seat-cushion ties such as these: they are an important decorative finishing touch and need to be long enough to tie in a pretty bow.
- Be bold with your choice of fabrics, and introduce some color contrasts in the patchwork pieces; if everything harmonizes perfectly, the result can look a little bland.

1 Place the foam on the chair seat, and cut it to fit, slicing through it with a sharp craft knife. Round off the corners so that the pad follows the contours of the seat. Fold the pattern paper, and place it on the seat so that the fold lies along the halfway point on the cushion pad. Draw the pattern piece to fit the pad, adding an extra ¾ inch around the outside edges for the seam allowance.

2 Using the template on page 121, make a paper pattern for the patchwork triangles. Cut out fourteen triangles using a selection of the patchwork fabrics. Right sides together and taking a ½-inch seam, pin and then stitch seven triangles together to form a long strip, trimming and pressing the seams open as you go. Make another strip of seven triangles in the same way.

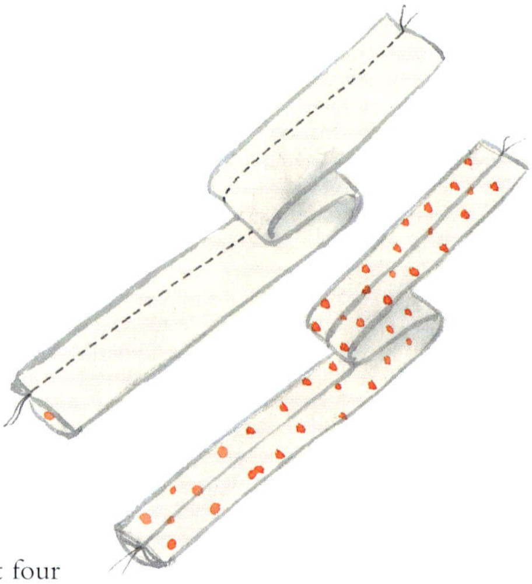

5 For the seat cushion ties, cut four strips of fabric measuring 3 x 16½ inches, following the grain of the fabric. Fold the first strip in half lengthwise, right sides together, and stitch along one short edge and then down the long edge, taking a ½-inch seam. Trim the seam, turn right side out, and press flat with the seam in the center of the tie. Make three more ties in the same way.

6 Place the patchwork on top of the interlining and both of these layers on top of the calico backing, matching the edges. Baste the layers together, and machine-stitch straight lines to zigzag across the ticking bands. Thread a needle with a double strand of embroidery floss, and starting from the patchwork side, stitch through the center of each triangle, leaving about 1 inch of floss protruding on the top. Bring the needle back up to the top, and then down and back up again once more. Knot the floss on the top side, and trim the ends to ½ inch.

3 Cut three strips of ticking measuring 20 x 3½ inches. Trim the edges of the patchwork strips straight. Right sides together, pin a strip of ticking to the long edges of a patchwork strip. Stitch together, taking a ½-inch seam. Pin the second patchwork strip to the other long edge of the ticking band, and stitch as before. Stitch the other two strips of ticking to each side of the patchwork strips to form bands along the top and bottom edges of the seat cushion. Trim and press open the seams.

4 Pin the paper pattern piece to the assembled patchwork and ticking so that the central band of ticking runs across the middle of the seat cushion, and cut around it. Using the same paper pattern, cut one piece of interlining, one piece of calico, and one piece of patterned fabric for the bottom of the cushion.

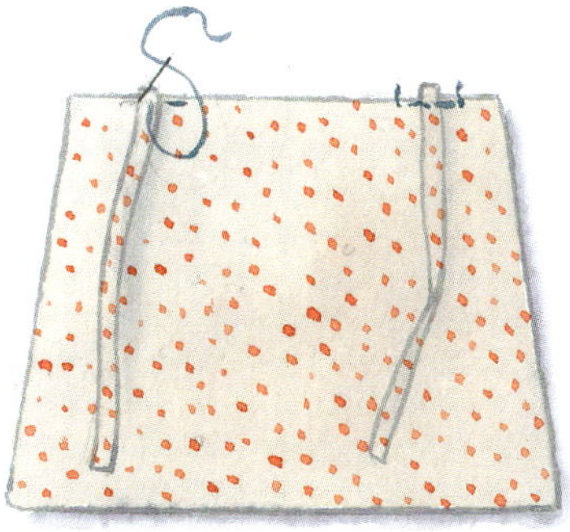

7 Following the instructions on page 118, make a strip of corded piping 52 inches long. Pin and baste the corded piping in place around the edge of the seat cushion with the raw edge facing outward. (See step 6, page 100.) Pin and baste a tie to the right side of the backing fabric along the top edge of the seat-cushion bottom piece approximately 2 inches in from the side edge, adjusting the position to suit the back of your own chair. Position another tie in the same position on the other side of the top edge.

8 Right sides together, pin the seat-cushion bottom to the quilted top, and stitch along the top edge, taking a ¾-inch seam and leaving the central 10 inches open. Press the seam open, and baste the zipper into the opening. Machine-stitch in place using a zipper foot attachment. Open the zipper. Pin the remaining two ties along the side edges of the seat-cushion bottom approximately 1 inch down from the back edge. Machine-stitch around the remaining three sides, using a zipper foot and stitching as close as possible to the piping cord. Turn the cover right side out, and remove any basting stitches. Insert the foam cushion pad.

Similar shades of red unite this bold mix of patterned fabrics.

bedroom curtain with flying-geese border

Based on a traditional pattern known as Flying Geese, repeating triangles make an effective patchwork border for curtain panels. The border can be adapted to fit any size curtain and makes a sumptuous edging when a pair of panels is closed. The bound edge of the top of the curtain is designed to be seen and will look great hanging from wood or metal rings and a curtain pole. A lightweight curtain for a bedroom or kitchen doesn't need any padding—just front and backing fabrics, with no interlining in between. For heavier panels to help keep the room warm over the winter months, you could add a layer of batting to provide some insulation.

YOU WILL NEED

Scraps of small-patterned and mid-toned fabrics for the main patchwork triangles

Scraps of a light-toned fabric for the side patchwork triangles

Lightweight linen, the length of your window plus 1 inch by 1½ times the width of your curtain (see left)

Cotton fabric for backing, the same size as the linen

Enough rickrack braid or other decorative trim to fit the length of the curtain

Enough fabric to make binding to fit all around the curtain

Curtain heading tape

Medium-sized colored buttons (optional)

STRONG SHAPES AND PATTERNS
The "flying geese" stand out boldly against their cream-colored background, while the pale blue linen used for the bulk of the curtain provides subtle color without overpowering the patchwork.

TIPS

- For a lightweight curtain, a simple gathered heading tape is suitable; the fabric should be 1½ to two times the width of the window.
- For heavier panels, use pencil-pleat tape; the fabric should be two to 2½ times the width of the window.

1 First work out how many patchwork bands you will need to make up the border that runs the length of the curtain. Each finished band is 3 inches deep, so divide the length of the curtain by this amount. Using the templates on page 123, cut one triangle 1 from patterned fabric and two triangle 2 pieces from your chosen light-toned solid-color fabric for each band. Right sides together and taking a ¼-inch seam, machine-stitch one triangle 2 piece to each short side of triangle 1. Press open the seams.

2 Make up the required number of patchwork bands in the same way, and arrange them in a pleasing pattern. Right sides together and taking a ¼-inch seam, machine-stitch them together to make the patchwork strip that runs the length of the curtain.

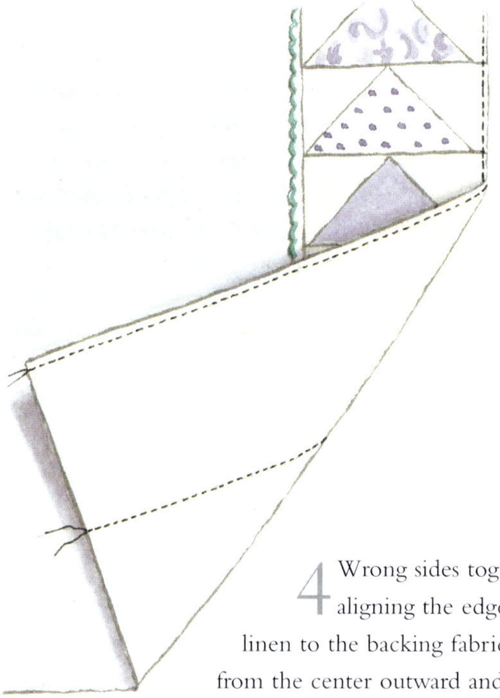

4 Wrong sides together and aligning the edges, pin the linen to the backing fabric, working from the center outward and smoothing out the fabric as you go. Machine-stitch down the sides of the patchwork border, following the seam line on the inside edge and stitching ¼ inch in from the outside edge. Machine-stitch along the other three sides of the curtain in the same way.

5 Cut strips of the binding fabric 2½ inches wide, and join them together to make a piece long enough to fit around all four sides of the curtain. Fold under ½ inch along one long edge of the binding, and press. With the right side of the binding to the back of the curtain, pin the raw edge of the binding all the way around the edge, and machine-stitch it in place, taking a ½-inch seam and mitering the corners. (See page 119.) Fold the binding over to the right side of the curtain so that the folded edge meets the line of stitching, and pin it in place. Topstitch close to the edge of the binding to secure.

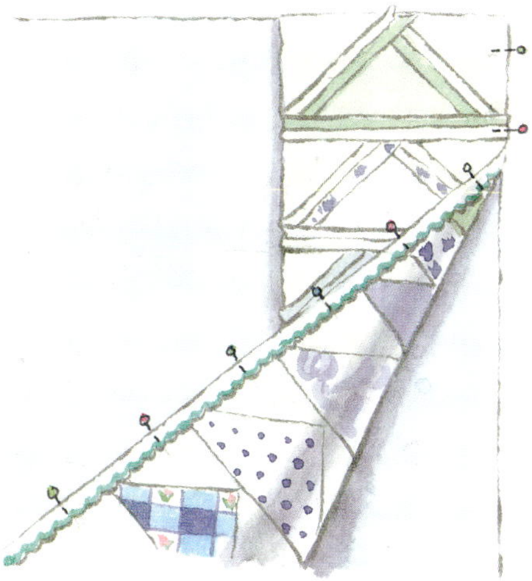

3 Cut away a 7-inch strip down the edge of the linen fabric that will become the bordered edge of the curtain. Pin a length of decorative trim to the long edge of the patchwork band that will be joined to the curtain. Right sides together and taking a ¼-inch seam, machine-stitch the band to the edge of the curtain. Press the seam flat.

6 Stitch curtain heading tape to the back of the curtain. Stitch a button to the apex of each large patterned triangle, stitching through all layers, to complete.

Colorful buttons that complement both the patchwork fabrics and the polka-dot edging provide an attractive, handcrafted finishing touch.

country-style curtain

Thick, interlined curtains are warm and sumptuous—just what you need during the fall and winter months to provide your home with additional insulation. Using quilts as curtains is practical as well as visually satisfying: a bed quilt or sofa throw can be hung at the window for the colder months and returned to its original purpose for the rest of the year. Here, a country-style curtain has been made from staggered rectangles of checkered fabrics—cottons, flannels, and fine wool. A length of crochet edging gives a delicate edge to the curtain, with the quilting at the outer edges making a channeled border all the way around.

The curtain measures 38 x 60 inches. Adjust to fit your own window. The quantities given are for a single curtain.

YOU WILL NEED

Scraps of fabrics 6 inches wide for the patchwork
60 inches of 55-inch-wide fabric for the backing
60 inches of 55-inch-wide cotton interlining
Embroidery floss
20 inches of 36-inch-wide fabric for the edging
Curtain heading tape and curtain hooks
60 inches of crochet edging

TIP

This is a great way of using up odds and ends left over from other sewing projects—or even recycling old jackets and skirts that have seen better days. However, try to make sure that all of the fabrics you use are roughly the same weight.

COZY COLORS
Warm reds predominate in this country-style curtain—just the thing for keeping out the drafts on cold winter nights.

1 Cut rectangles 6 inches wide from your selected fabrics, varying the lengths to suit the fabrics you have. Right sides together, pin two rectangles together along one 6-inch edge, and machine-stitch, taking a ½-inch seam. Press open the seam. Continue to join rectangles together in the same way to make long strips of different-sized rectangles.

2 Lay the strips on the floor side by side, and cut them to the length you need your curtain to be. Right sides together, pin two strips together along one long edge, and machine-stitch as before, pressing the seam open. Continue adding strips in the same way until you reach the required width.

4 Work two evenly spaced rows of quilting stitches by machine or by hand within both end strips of rectangles and at the same spacing across the top and bottom of the piece. Tie-quilt through the fabrics at random intervals over some of the rectangle corners to hold the layers of fabric together. (See page 118.) Remove the pins and basting stitches.

5 Cut strips of edging fabric 2¾ inches wide to make the binding, and stitch them together into a continuous strip to fit the length of all four sides of the curtain. Right sides together with edging ¾ inch in from edge of backing fabric, machine-stitch the binding strip to the backing fabric 1 inch in from the edge, and trim the ends to align with the backing and interlining. Fold the binding to the front; turn under ½ inch along the raw edge; and pin it so that it overlaps the edge rectangles on the quilt top. Machine-stitch it in place.

3 Lay the backing fabric right side down with the interlining on top; then center the assembled patchwork right side up on the interlining. Cut the interlining and backing fabrics so that they extend ¾ inch beyond the patchwork on all sides. Working from the center outward, pin and then baste all the layers together.

6 Bind the top and bottom edges of the curtain in the same way, extending the binding by ½ inch at each end. Fold the ½-inch extension to the inside when folding the binding over, and slip-stitch the folded ends to close them at each edge. Machine-stitch a length of heading tape along the back of the curtain top, and then slip-stitch the crochet edging along the inside edge of the curtain to complete.

A strip of crochet edging adds a delicate, decorative finishing touch.

CHAPTER 4

Bags and Gifts

Patchwork and quilted accessories are all the rage, with top-quality fashion and homeware designers incorporating these age-old quilter's techniques into their contemporary collections. This chapter features a range of small-scale decorative items, from stylish bags that every fashion-conscious girl about town would love to own to pretty little gifts for your family and friends.

SPECIAL HANDBAG
Only machine stitches will give the strength this charming but practical bag needs so you can use it every day.

special handbag

Pretty cotton fabric is the starting point for creating a lightweight, textured fashion accessory. Machine stitches make the bag sturdy, while the patchwork pattern and pearl-button detail set the style.

The finished handbag is 8 inches high and 8½ inches wide.

YOU WILL NEED

- *A selection of cotton and linen fabric scraps for the patchwork*
- *4-inch strip of 36-inch-wide linen for the side gussets and base*
- *10 inches of 36-inch-wide fabric for the lining*
- *12 inches of 44-inch-wide interlining*
- *24 small pearl buttons and one large button*
- *2 yards of 1-inch grosgrain ribbon*
- *4 inches of ½-inch-wide ribbon*

TIPS

- Intersperse patterned fabrics with solid colors so that the effect of the prints is not completely overpowering.
- Repeat one of the patterned fabrics for the bag lining, to create visual continuity.

PRETTY SOPHISTICATED

The simplest of decorations can transform an ordinary bag into something infinitely more sophisticated and splendid. Here, pearl buttons add a touch of glamour.

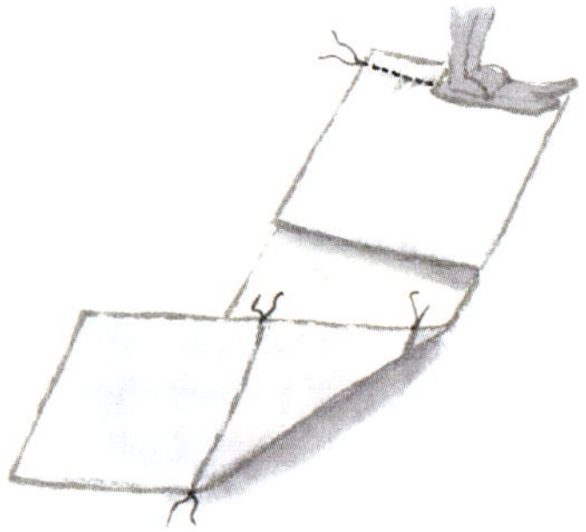

1 Cut out forty 2¾-inch squares in a variety of patterned fabrics to make the patchwork. Lay out the squares in four rows of five squares for both the back and front of the bag, arranging the colors and patterns randomly. Right sides together and taking a ½-inch seam, stitch the squares together row by row, trimming and pressing the seams open as you go. Then join the rows together, taking care to align the seams, again trimming and pressing the seams open as you go.

2 Cut two pieces of interlining the same size as the patchwork pieces. Place the front of the bag on one piece, right side up, and baste the two layers together. Sew a small pearl button at every square intersection on the right side. Repeat for the back of the bag.

5 Turn the bag right side out, and place the lining inside the patchwork bag. Turn the seam allowances to the wrong side along the top of the side gussets and corresponding lining pieces and up the sides of the bag, and slip-stitch the three edges together on both sides. Baste the raw edges together along the top of the bag on both back and front.

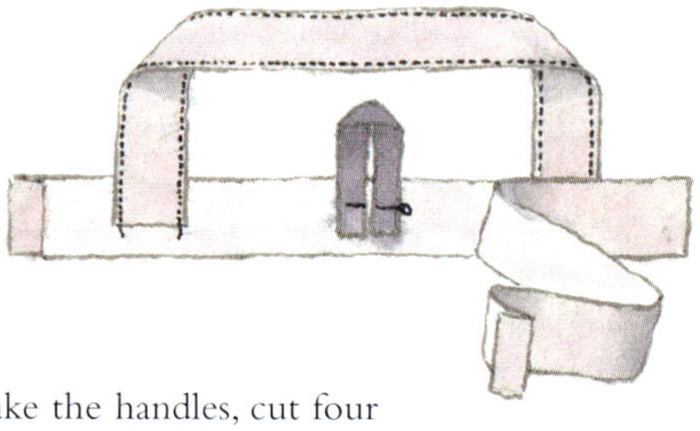

6 To make the handles, cut four pieces of grosgrain ribbon 8½ inches long. Place them together in pairs, wrong sides together, and machine-stitch together close to the edges. Make a button loop by folding the strip of ½-inch ribbon in half lengthwise, and stitch down the long open edge. Cut to 3 inches long, and fold in half. For the top binding, cut four strips of grosgrain ribbon 8 inches long, and fold in ½ inch along all short ends. Wrong sides together, place the grosgrain ribbon strips together in pairs, pinning the button loop into the center of one of the pairs. Tuck the ends of the handles between them, and machine-stitch close to the edges along both short sides and one long side.

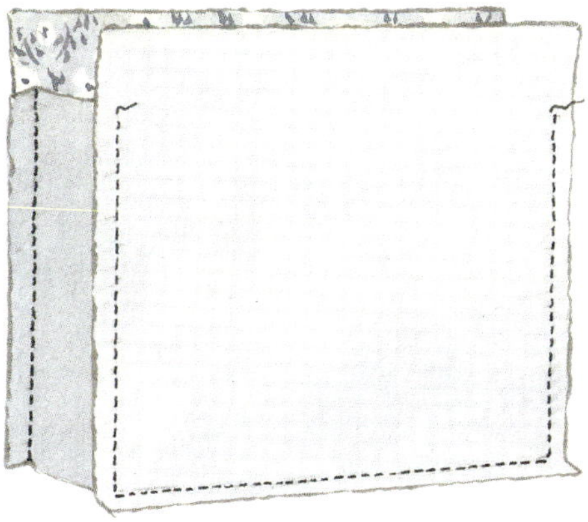

3 For the side gussets, cut two linen rectangles measuring 7 x 2½ inches. For the base, cut a linen rectangle measuring 9¾ x 2½ inches. Right sides together, pin and then stitch a side-gusset piece to each short edge of the base, taking ½-inch seams but leaving ½ inch unstitched at both ends of each seam. Press the seams flat. Right sides together, pin the side-gusset and base-gusset strips along the base and up the sides of one of the patchwork pieces, using the open ends on the base-gusset seams to turn the corners, and stitch it, leaving ½ inch open at both ends. Join the other patchwork piece in the same way. Turn right side out, and press.

4 From the lining fabric, cut two rectangles for the front and back measuring 8 x 9¾ inches, two side gussets measuring 7 x 2½ inches, and a base gusset measuring 9¾ x 2½ inches. Right sides together, pin and then stitch the lining together in the same way as you joined the pieces in step 3, using the open seam ends to turn the bottom corners. Press the seams.

7 Lightly gather the top edges of the bag to fit inside the top binding. Baste the binding and handles in place so that the grosgrain overlaps the gathered edge along the top of the bag and the edges match on the outside and inside of the bag. Machine-stitch through all thicknesses close to the ribbons' edges to complete. Stitch the large button in position on the bag front to correspond with the button loop.

A large button closure secures the bag, while small pearl buttons add flair.

travel tote

This handy sized travel tote is practical as well as funky. Smart enough for a special occasion, it is also casual enough to use every day. Classic gingham checks in different sizes are offset by a 1950s' starburst fabric in blue, black, and cream. Blue canvas is used to edge and line the bag, with spotted ribbon in black and white providing a graphic trim for the handles and bag top. Each square is contour-quilted, with a machine-stitched line inside each square forming a padded frame. The quilting makes a soft, squishy bag that will keep its contents safe and cushioned. Contour quilting is easy to do and is a good technique to do by machine.

The tote measures 14 x 12 inches.

YOU WILL NEED

Scraps of three different fabrics for the patchwork
16 inches of 55-inch-wide cotton canvas for the lining and handles
16 inches of 55-inch-wide cotton interlining
55 inches of ½-inch ribbon
Approximately 40 inches of bias binding (optional)
Matching sewing threads

BOLD BLUES AND BLACKS
The regularity of the gingham checks is offset by the more-random patterning of the black starbursts and cream polka dots.

TIP

Contour quilting relies on regularly spaced lines for its effect. If you're not confident about your ability to stitch in a straight line, place a strip of ½-inch masking tape around the outer edge of each square and machine-stitch alongside it.

1 Cut 24 4½-inch squares from the patchwork fabrics. Make the front of the traveling bag by arranging 12 of the squares in a pleasing pattern, four squares across and three squares deep. Right sides together and taking ½-inch seams, machine-stitch the first row of four squares together. Press the seams flat. Make two more rows of four squares in the same way.

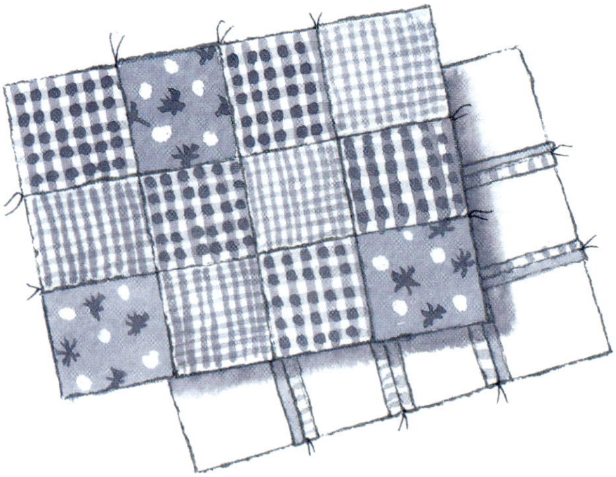

2 Right sides together and taking ½-inch seams, machine-stitch the three rows together to make a rectangle, aligning the seams carefully. Press the seams open. Join the remaining 12 squares in the same way to make the back of the bag.

5 Contour-quilt each of the patchwork squares, on both the front and back of the bag by topstitching through all layers ½ inch in from the edge of each square. Cut away ½ inch of the interlining along the sides and base edge of both front and back pieces.

6 Right sides together and matching the edges, pin the front and back together. Machine-stitch around the sides and base, taking a ½-inch seam. Press the seam open. Neaten the seam with a zigzag machine stitch, or bind the raw edges with bias binding. (See page 118.)

3 Place the cotton canvas right side down, with the interlining on top, aligning the edges. Place one patchwork rectangle on top of the interlining, with one long edge 1½ inches from the edge of the interlining. This edge will be the top of the bag. Pin the layers together, and cut out, cutting around the short sides and the base of the patchwork rectangle. Repeat for the back of the bag. Stitch a line through all the layers, ½ inch from the top edge of the patchwork.

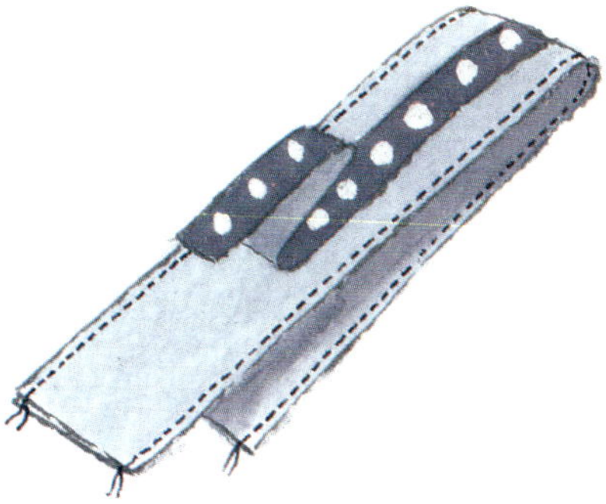

4 Cut two 3 x 11½-inch strips of canvas for the handles. On each one, press ½ inch to the wrong side along both long edges. Fold in half lengthwise, wrong sides together, and pin. Topstitch along both long edges, stitching as close to the edge as possible. Pin a length of ribbon down the center of the right side of each handle, and topstitch it in place along both edges.

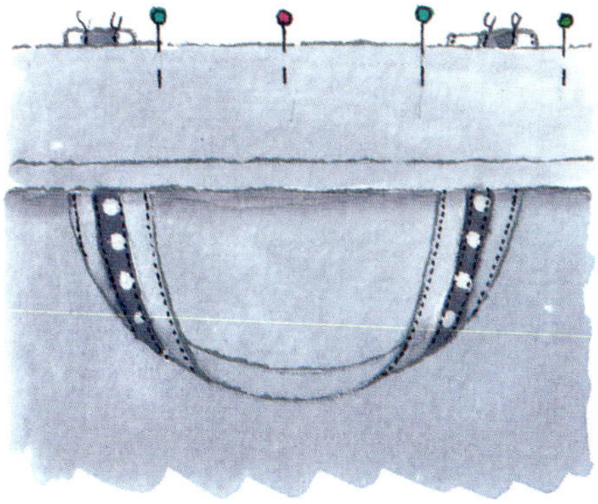

7 Cut two 2½ x 15-inch strips of canvas for the top band. Right sides together, pin the strips together at both short edges, and machine-stitch, taking a ½-inch seam. Press open the seams. Turn under, and press ½ inch to the wrong side along one raw edge. Pin the handles to the wrong side of the top edge of the traveling bag. With the right side of the top band to the wrong side of the bag, pin the band around the top of the bag, with the raw edges together and the handles sandwiched in between. Machine-stitch around the top edge, ½ inch from the edge, stitching through all layers.

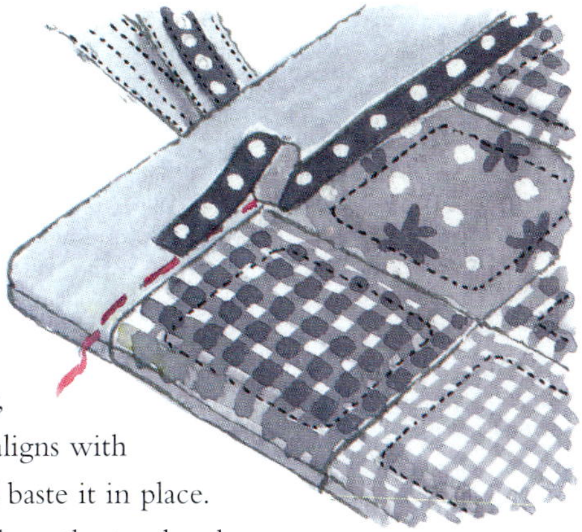

8 Turn the bag right side out. Turn the top band to the right side of the bag, so that the folded edge aligns with the line of stitching, and baste it in place. Pin a length of ribbon along the top band, so that the top edge just covers the folded edge of the top band, and topstitch it in place along both edges.

Spotted ribbon on the handles and around the top of the bag picks up the colors of the patchwork.

sewing-basket liner

A collection of old ties gets a new lease on life when they are used to make patchwork. The stunning, silky fabrics with small jacquard patterns work well in this way. Ties are usually quite narrow, so to make the most use of the fabric you will have to cut the seams that run down the back of each tie and open them out. Ties are always cut on the cross of the fabric, so there isn't a lot of fabric with which to play, but luckily this basket lining needs only small pieces. The diamond-patterned lid lining has extra padding, making it useful for storing needles and pins. You might also want to add a few pockets around the sides in which to store scissors, thimbles, and bobbins of thread.

The measurements given here are for a basket that is approximately 9½ inches deep x 6¼ inches wide x 3½ inches high. You may need to adjust the sizes to fit your own basket.

YOU WILL NEED

Scraps of fabric for the patchwork

8 x 12 inches of batting to line the lid

32 x 12 inches of backing fabric

Fabric adhesive

Toggle for the lid

32 inches of rickrack braid

32 x 12 inches of interlining for the base and sides

Dried rosemary leaves, thin piping cord, and narrow ribbon for the needle sharpener (optional)

TIP

Look for a basket with a fairly open weave so that you will be able to push a needle and thread through the sides to secure the lining to it. Wear a thimble to protect your fingers when you do this.

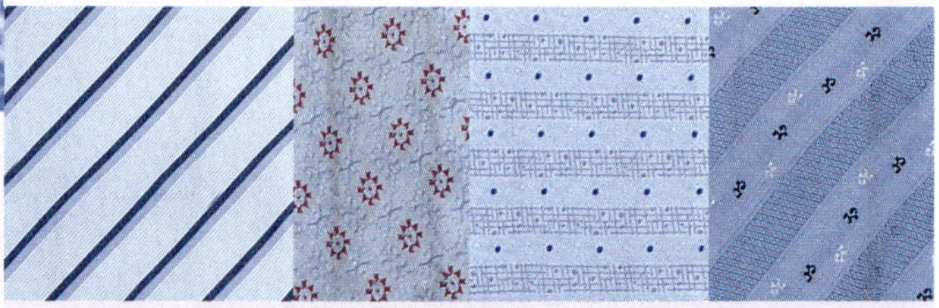

SILK SPLENDOR

Assorted small-patterned silk ties make a hard-wearing but sumptuous-looking lining for the sewing basket.

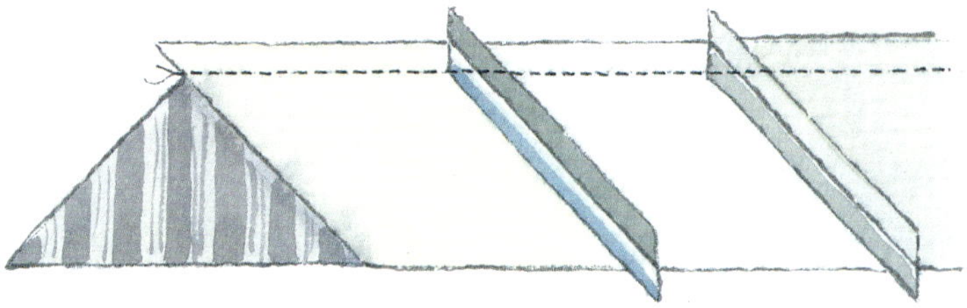

1 Using the template on page 121, cut twenty-two diamonds from the selection of patchwork fabrics. Lay the diamonds out in alternating rows of six and five diamonds, moving them around until you are happy with the arrangement. Right sides together, pin two diamonds together along one sloping edge, and machine-stitch them, taking a ¼-inch seam. Press open the seam. Continue joining diamonds together in this way until you have four rows.

2 Right sides together, pin two rows to each other along one long edge, aligning the seams, and machine-stitch, taking a ¼-inch seam. Press open the seam. Add the remaining two strips in the same way. Cut two 1 x 11-inch strips from one of the patchwork fabrics. Right sides together and taking a ¼-inch seam, stitch one strip along each long edge of the patchwork piece. Press open the seams. Cut out a 10¼ x 7-inch rectangle from the patchwork piece.

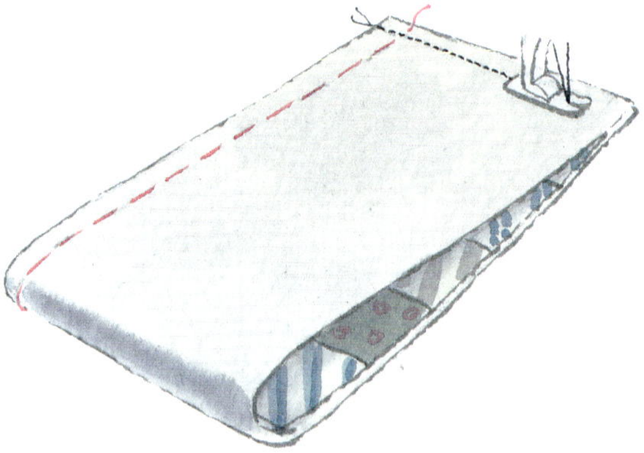

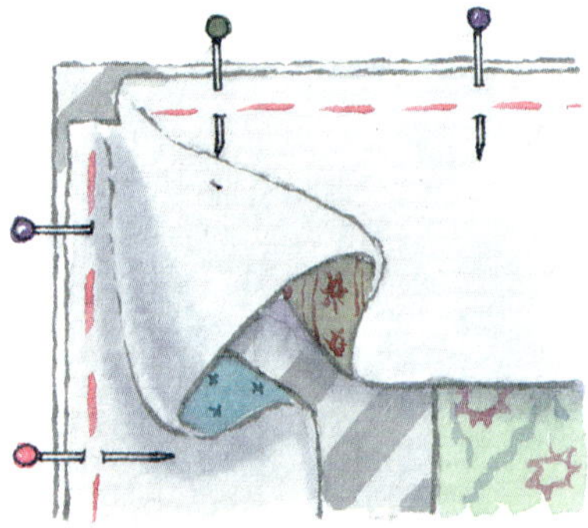

5 To line the sides of the basket, cut 13 3 x 4½-inch rectangles from the patchwork fabrics. Machine-stitch them together along their long edges, taking ¼-inch seams, to make a continuous strip. Press open the seams. Cut a piece of interlining and a piece of backing fabric to the same size as the patchwork. Place the patchwork right side up on top of the interlining, and pin the two pieces together. Place the backing fabric right side down on top of the patchwork; pin it along one long edge; and machine-stitch along this long edge, taking a ½-inch seam. Trim the seam, and fold the backing fabric over the interlining so that the interlining is sandwiched between the backing and the patchwork. Baste along the raw long edge, stitching through all layers. Cut away 1 inch from one short end of the strip. Right sides together and taking a ½-inch seam, machine-stitch the short edges of the strip together. Press the seam flat.

6 To line the base of the basket, machine-stitch five 6¾ x 3-inch rectangles of the patchwork fabric together along their long edges, as in step 5. Cut the completed patchwork to 10 x 6¾ inches. Place the backing fabric right side down, with the interlining on top and the patchwork right side up on top of the interlining. Right sides together, pin the side strip along the edge of the base, clipping into the seam allowance at the corners. Machine-stitch, taking a ½-inch seam.

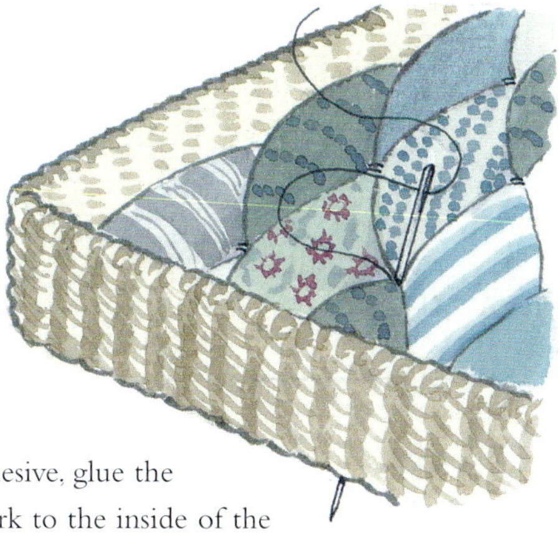

3 Cut a 10¼ x 7-inch piece of batting, and pin it to the wrong side of the patchwork. Cut a piece of backing fabric to the same size. Right sides together, pin the backing to the patchwork. Taking a ½-inch seam, machine-stitch around all four sides, leaving a gap of about 4 inches in one side. Trim the seam, turn right side out, and slip-stitch the gap closed. Press lightly to flatten the side seams.

4 Using fabric adhesive, glue the padded patchwork to the inside of the basket lid. Using a needle and strong thread, stitch through the patchwork and the basket lid in several places to give the lining its quilted look. Stitch a toggle to the outside of the lid. Glue a length of rickrack braid around the edge of the lid lining.

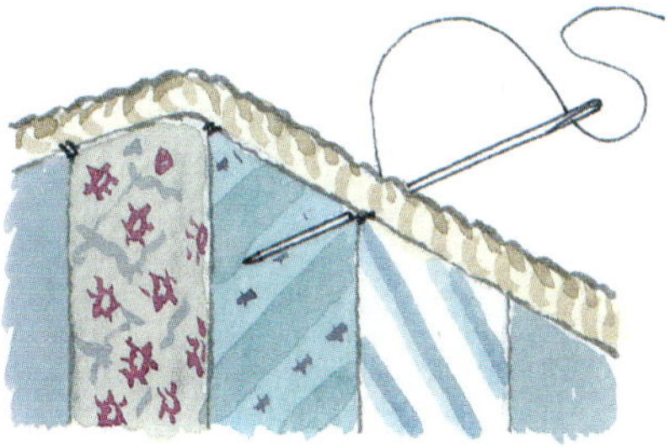

7 Place the lining inside the basket so that the corners line up. Using a needle and strong thread, make a few stitches at regular intervals around the top of the lining, stitching through all layers of the fabric and the basket to fix the lining in place.

8 To make the needle sharpener, cut two more diamonds, using the template on page 121. Right sides together and taking a ¼-inch seam, machine-stitch around the edges, leaving a gap of about ½ inch in one side. Turn right side out, stuff the diamond tightly with dried rosemary leaves, and slip-stitch the opening closed. Slip-stitch a length of piping cord around the edge of the diamond. Stitch a ribbon bow to the top point, and hand-stitch the diamond to the side of the basket lining.

This is a simple but effective way of keeping your needles sharp—dried rosemary leaves in a pretty, diamond-shaped cushion.

heart-motif pincushion

If you are new to patchwork and quilting, a small project such as this pincushion is an ideal one with which to start. It uses only two fabrics—one patterned and one solid-colored—and follows a simple patchwork block design to form the shape of a heart. The piped edging provides a finishing touch; I made it from the same fabric as the patchwork, but a store-bought ready-made piping or braid could be set into the seam just as well. Packaged together with some glass-headed pins and a pair of embroidery scissors, the pincushion would make the perfect gift for a budding seamstress.

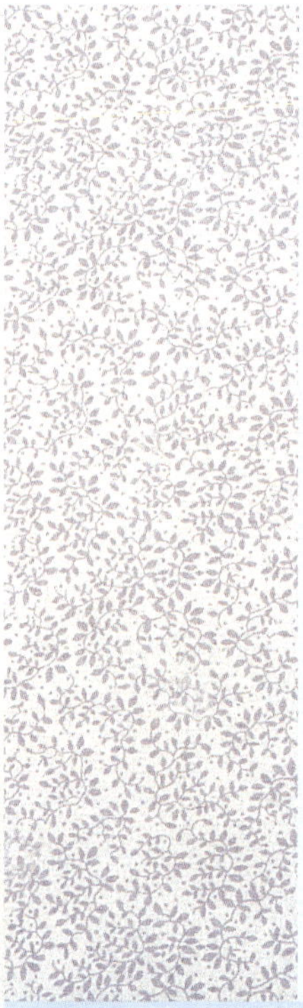

The finished pincushion is approximately 6½ inches square.

YOU WILL NEED

Scraps of solid-color cream or other light-colored fabric (fabric 1)

Scraps of patterned fabric (fabric 2)

10-inch square of interlining

10-inch square of backing fabric

10-inch square of cream or light-colored fabric for the cushion back

Approx. 28 inches of corded piping

Stuffing

Embroidery floss

CUTTING INSTRUCTIONS

Using the templates on page 124, cut the following number of fabric patches:

Template 1: two pieces from each fabric

Template 2: two pieces from fabric 2

Template 3: four pieces from fabric 1

Template 4: two pieces from fabric 2

THE QUILTER'S FRIEND
Ideal as a gift for a new generation of quilters, the sturdy fabric of this pincushion makes sure it keeps its shape.

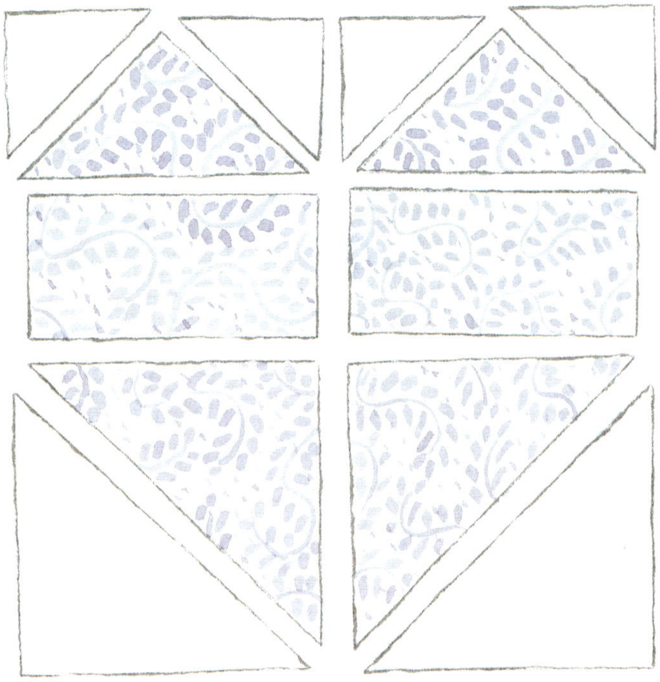

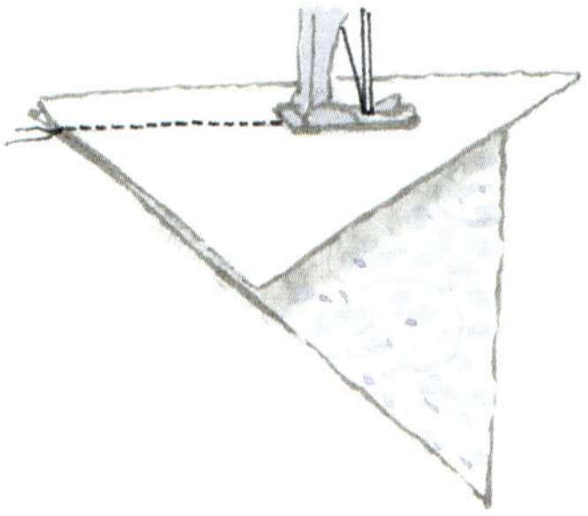

2 Right sides together, pin a template 3 triangle to one side of a template 4 triangle, and machine-stitch, taking a ¼-inch seam. Press the seam open; then sew another template 3 triangle to the other side of the template 4 triangle. Press the seam open, and trim the sides straight.

1 Following the diagram above, lay out the fabric pieces in the correct order.

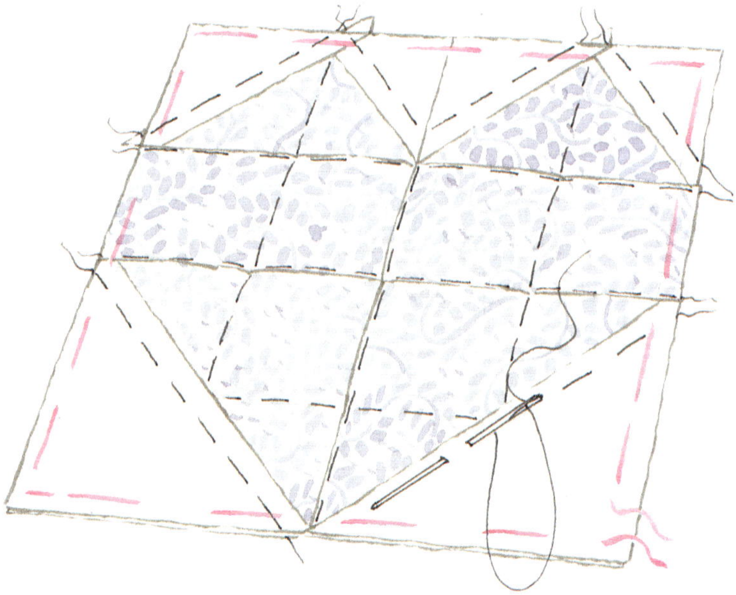

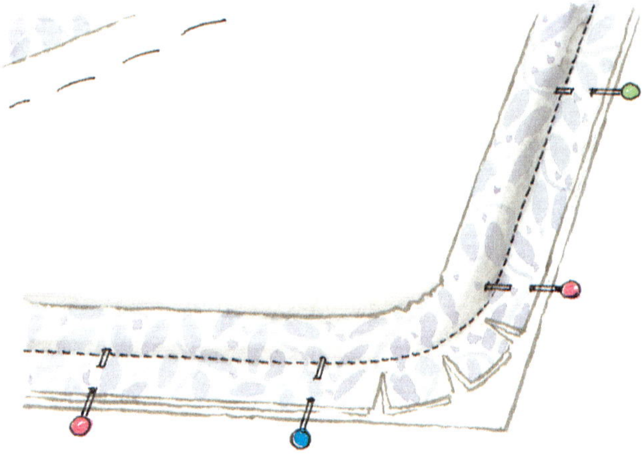

5 Using embroidery floss, quilt by hand, using small running stitches so that rows of stitches run parallel to the edges of the heart on the plain fabric and the patterned heart has lines of stitching that divide it into quarters. Remove the basting stitches.

6 Cut the fabric for the back of the pincushion to the same size as the patchwork front. Following the instructions on page 118, make enough corded piping to go around the edge of the pincushion. Pin it to the right side of the patchwork with the raw edges facing outward, snipping the seam allowance on the piping to turn the corners. Join the ends. (See page 118.)

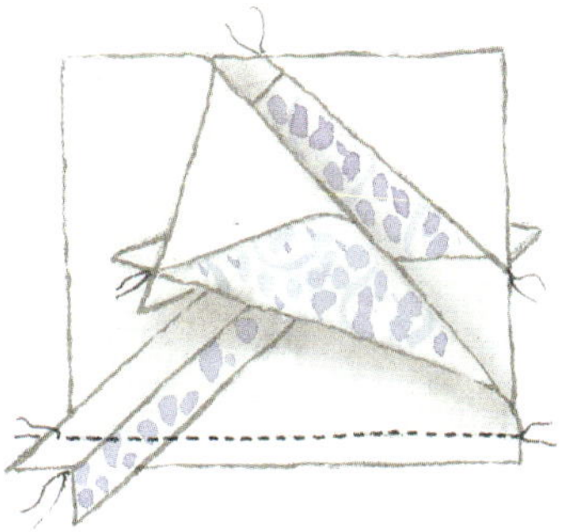

3 Right sides together, pin one patterned and one solid-colored template 1 triangle together. Machine-stitch, taking a ¼-inch seam. Press open the seam. Right sides together, pin and machine-stitch a template 2 patch along the base of the template 4 patch from step 2. Stitch the other side of the template 2 patch to the pieced template 1 triangles. Press open the seams. This forms half of the heart. Repeat steps 2 and 3 to make the other half. Right sides together, stitch the two halves of the heart together.

4 Lay the interlining on top of the backing fabric and the patchwork pincushion front on top of the interlining, and pin all the layers together. Trim the edges to match all the way around. Baste the layers together.

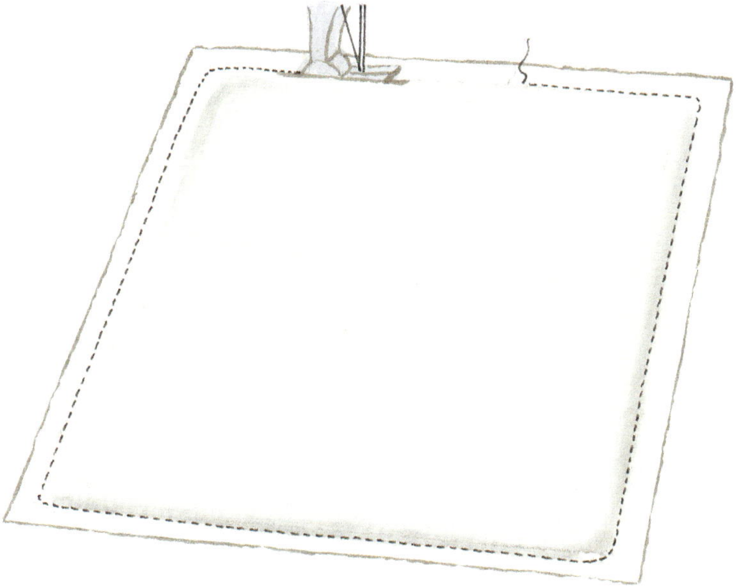

7 Right sides together, pin the patchwork front and the cushion back together. Using a piping foot and stitching as close as possible to the piping cord, stitch the back and front together, leaving an opening of about 2 inches along one edge. Turn the cushion right side out. Stuff firmly, and slip-stitch the gap closed.

Trim the pincushion with piping cord covered in the same fabric as the heart for a coordinating finishing touch.

lavender sachet

The design for this lavender sachet is a simple patchwork block pattern made up of nine squares. Only small fabric scraps are required, and, in this instance, fine linen handkerchiefs and fabric remnants found at tag sales are used. The lavender inside the sachet is in its own muslin bag, which means it can be replenished from time to time to refresh the perfume. The back of the sachet has a buttoned fastening, so it is easy to change the inner bag.

The finished sachet is approximately 8 inches square.

YOU WILL NEED

Scraps of six fabrics (A—F) for the patchwork
10-inch square of backing fabric
Embroidery floss
Five pearl buttons
18 x 14-inch piece of fabric for the sachet back
Three small buttons for the back of the sachet
8 x 16-inch piece of muslin or organdie for the lavender bag
Dried lavender flowers

CUTTING INSTRUCTIONS

Using the templates on page 124, cut out the following fabric patches:

Template 1: four pieces each of fabrics D and E, and one of fabric F

Template 2: four patches from fabric A and 16 pieces each of fabrics B and C

SWEET SCENTS

This delicately scented lavender sachet will keep your clothes-drawer fragrant. You could substitute rose petals if you prefer.

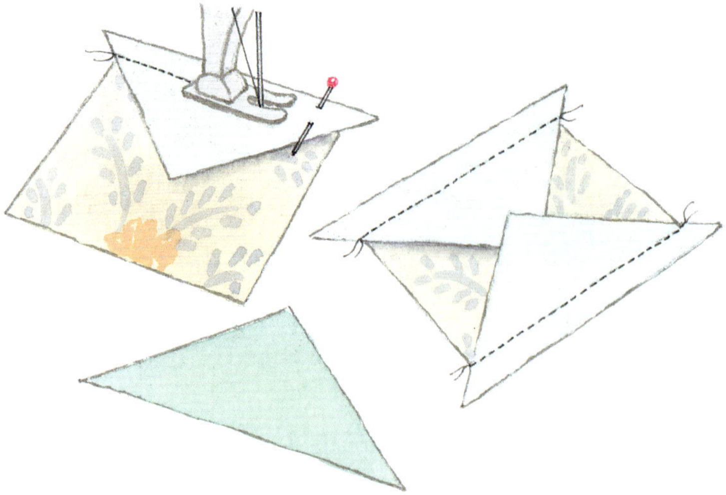

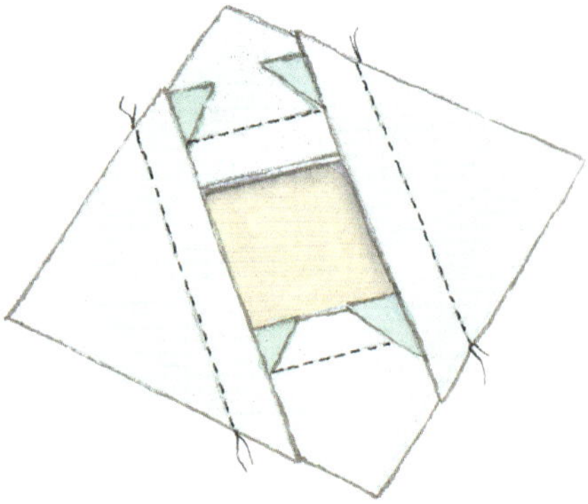

1 Right sides together, pin a triangle to one side of a square, and machine-stitch, taking a ¼-inch seam. Join another triangle of the same fabric to the opposite side of the square. Press the seams toward the center of the square.

2 Sew two more triangles of the same fabric to the other two sides of the square, and press the seams toward the center. This completes one square. Make up the other eight squares in the same way. Trim side edges straight.

5 Using embroidery thread, work rows of small running stitches to quilt the layers together, working diagonally across the squares in both directions. Alternatively, machine-stitch the layers together. Stitch a pearl button in the center of the corner and center squares.

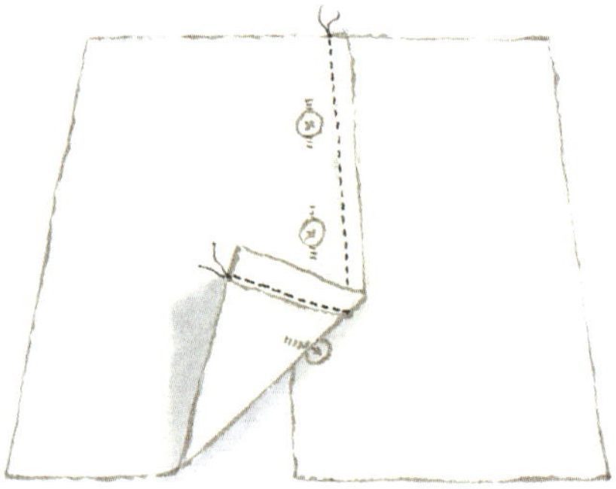

6 Cut two pieces of fabric measuring 8¼ x 6 inches for the sachet back. Make a hem along one short edge of each piece, turning ½ inch and then ¾ inch to the wrong side. Machine-stitch the hem in place. Evenly space three buttonholes along the hemmed edge of one of the back pieces. Overlap the two backing pieces so that the backing matches the patchwork front, and stitch the buttons in place. Right sides together and taking ¼-inch seams, machine-stitch together the patchwork front to the buttoned side. Turn right side out, and press the seams.

3 Join the squares together in three rows of three; then join the rows together to make the complete block of nine squares. Press all seams flat.

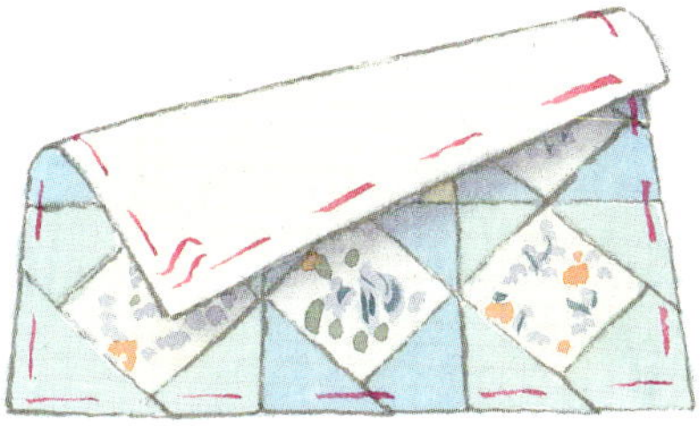

4 Cut the backing fabric to the same size as the patchwork block. Place the patchwork on the backing fabric; pin it in place; and baste the two layers together.

7 Using pinking shears, cut two 7½-inch squares of muslin. Pin the squares together, and machine-stitch around all sides, leaving an opening of about 2 inches along one side. Fill the bag with dried lavender, and stitch the opening closed. Place the bag inside the sachet.

Natural buttons are an attractive way of closing the sachet.

star-patterned laundry bag

This lightly quilted laundry bag is a stylish way of storing clothing destined for the laundry room that you want to keep out of sight. The front of the bag consists of a patchwork star block made up of a geometric pattern of squares and triangles, which is ideally suited to machine piecing. The same block would look wonderful repeated several times to make a full-sized quilt. Using remnants of cotton and linen in a subtle color scheme of cream, pink, and beige, the only patterned fabrics are a shirt stripe used in the patchwork and another wider stripe in two shades of pink for the top and back of the bag.

The finished laundry bag measures 16 x 23 inches.

YOU WILL NEED

Scraps of four fabrics for the patchwork (A = striped; B = pink linen; C = dark beige or taupe; D = light beige)

Four 1¼ x 17-inch strips of fabric D to edge the patchwork

For the back of the bag: 17 x 27¾ inches of fabric E (pale pink stripe)

For the bag front top: 17 x 10½ inches of fabric E

Two 17 x 19½-inch pieces of lining fabric

Embroidery floss

Approx. 1 yard of cord or tape for the drawstring

Matching sewing threads

CUTTING INSTRUCTIONS

Using the templates on page 125, cut the following number of fabric patches:

Template 1: 4 patches from fabric A

Template 2: 4 patches from fabric A

Template 3: 8 patches from fabric B

Template 4: 4 patches from fabric C, 1 patch from fabric E

Template 5: 8 patches from fabric A, 8 patches from fabric D

STARS AND STRIPES

The color scheme of cream, pink, and beige is subtle, but the striped fabric gives the piece a contemporary flavor.

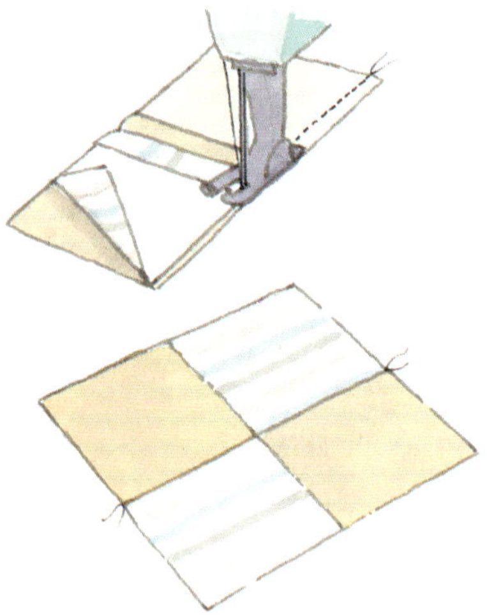

1 Using the template 5 pieces, assemble the small pieced squares for the patchwork block, taking ¼-inch seams and alternating the fabrics as shown. Press open the seams.

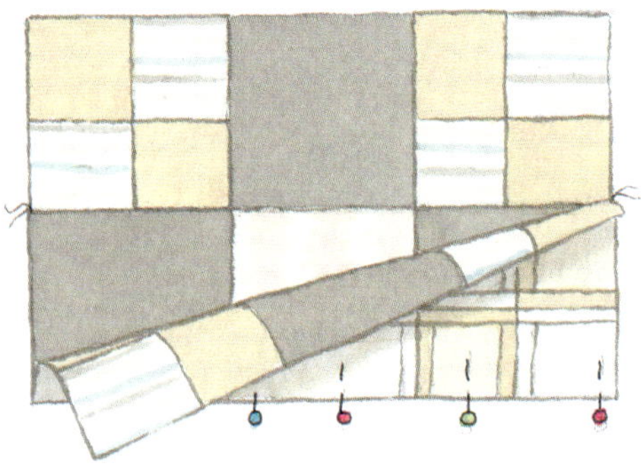

2 Again taking ¼-inch seams, machine-stitch one template 4 C piece between two of the pieced squares made in step 1 to make a row of three squares. Repeat to make a second row. Machine-stitch the template 4 E piece between the two remaining fabric D squares to make a third row of three squares. Press open the seams. Join the rows together, as shown, to complete the central block.

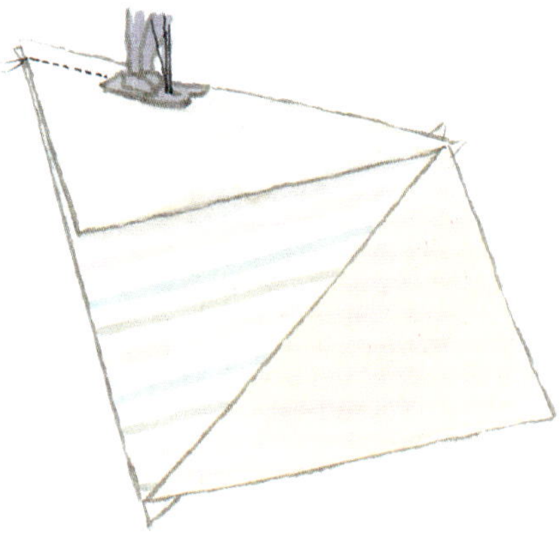

3 Machine-stitch one pink linen triangle to each side of a large, striped triangle, as shown, and join this rectangular strip to the top edge of the central block. Repeat along the bottom edge of the central block. Press open the seams.

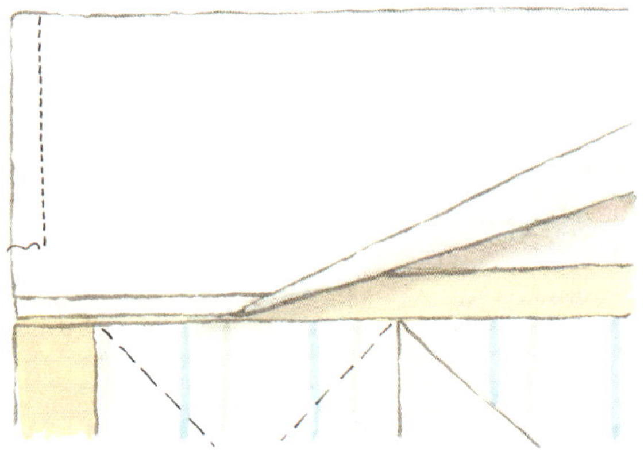

6 Wrong sides together, place the bag back and lining together, matching the bottom and side edges, and baste the fabrics together. Right sides together, pin and then stitch the bag front to the bag back along the bottom edge only, taking a ½-inch seam. Neaten the raw edges along the side and bottom edges with a zigzag machine stitch. Along both top edges, turn under a hem of ½ inch to the wrong side, and press. Fold the top of the bag front over by 4 inches. Machine-stitch the sides, taking ½-inch seams, stopping the stitching 1 inch from the folded edge. Repeat on the back of the bag.

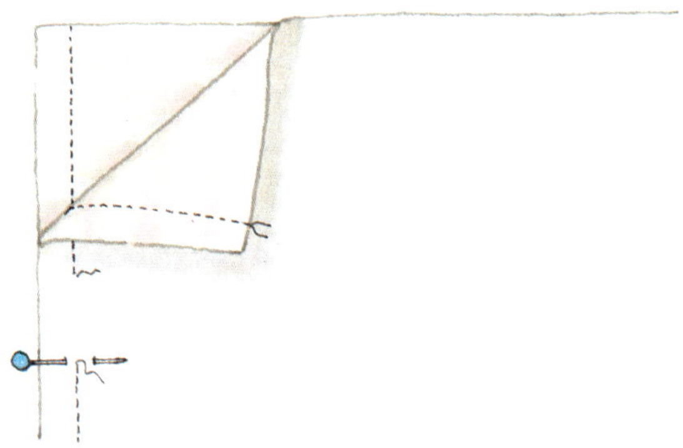

7 Right sides together and taking a ½-inch seam, machine-stitch the bag front to the back along the side edges, matching the top edges and stopping the stitching just short of the folded bag top. Turn the bag and the top edges right side out, and press the seams.

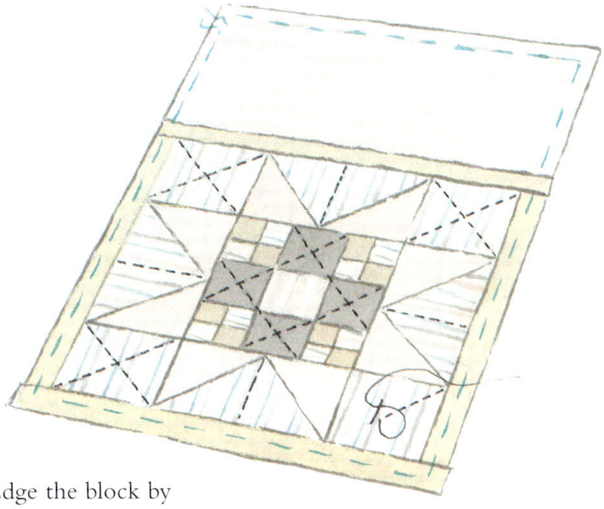

5 Edge the block by sewing a strip of fabric D to each side edge of the block, and trim away any excess fabric to match the block edges. Sew the other two strips of fabric D along the top and bottom edges of the block. Right sides together, pin the bag front top piece of fabric to the top of the patchwork block, and stitch together, taking a ½-inch seam. Press open the seam. Wrong sides together, lay the bag front on one piece of lining fabric, matching the bottom and side edges, and baste the fabrics together. Hand- or machine-quilt the patchwork through both layers of fabric, as shown.

4 Make the two side rectangular sections in the same way as in step 3, and machine-stitch a template 1 corner square to each end of each rectangle to complete the side sections. Stitch these side sections to each side of the central block, matching seams to complete the block.

The stripes on the border point inward, toward the central star block.

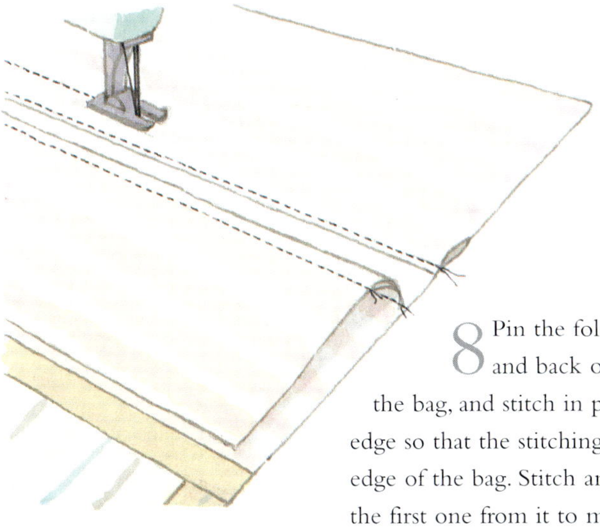

8 Pin the folded top edges on the front and back of the bag to the inside of the bag, and stitch in place close to the pressed edge so that the stitching is parallel with the top edge of the bag. Stitch another line parallel with the first one from it to make a channel for the drawcord on both the bag front and back. Thread through the drawcord, and knot the ends together.

padded hanger

Padded clothes hangers ensure that fabric isn't pulled out of shape when a garment is stored in the closet and that no ugly marks are left on the shoulders. Quilting is the perfect technique to use to make a padded hanger—and it looks great as well. Here, every scrap of a linen table runner has been put to use to make a unique hanger cover. Lines of embroidery on the fabric follow the lines of the hanger, and a scalloped edging on the cloth becomes an attractive decorative hem. Substitute your own special finds to create a one-of-a-kind piece.

NO STITCHING REQUIRED!
The scalloped, embroidered edge of an antique linen table runner makes an attractive, ready-made decorative hem.

The padded hanger is made to fit over a standard 16-inch wooden clothes hanger.

YOU WILL NEED

12 inches of 36-inch-wide linen

8 x 9½-inch piece of medium-weight batting

8 x 9½-inch piece of backing fabric

Three buttons

Embroidered motif or ribbon (optional)

16-inch wooden clothes hanger

CUTTING INSTRUCTIONS

Using the template on page 122, make a paper pattern for the main section of the hanger. Pin the pattern piece against a fold, and following the grain of the fabric, cut out two pieces. For the border, if you are using a hemmed-edge fabric from an old place mat, cut out four strips measuring 8¾ x 2¼ inches; if you are using an unhemmed piece of fabric, cut four strips measuring 9½ x 2¾ inches.

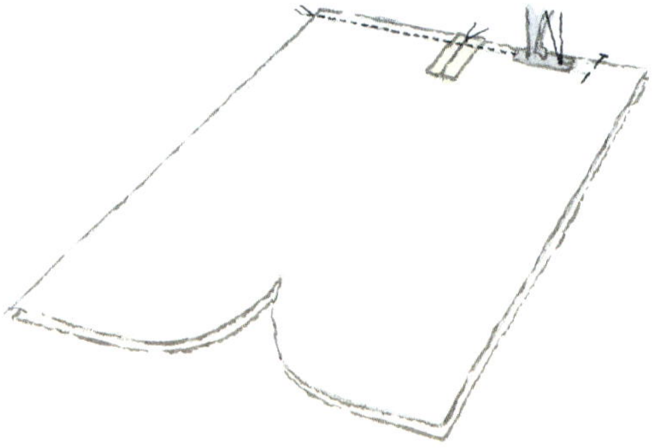

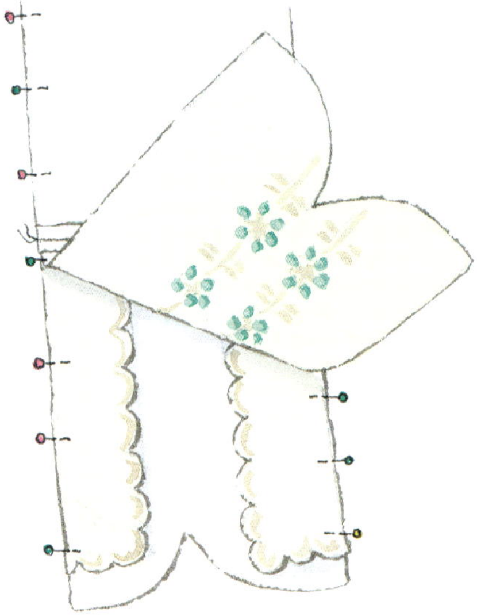

1 Right sides together, pin the two main hanger sections together along the short center edge, and machine-stitch together, taking a ½-inch seam. Press the seam open. Join the border strips in pairs along a short edge in the same way, and press open the seams. If the borders are not already hemmed, turn under ¼ inch followed by a further ¼ inch along both short edges and along one long edge of both border pieces. Machine-stitch the hems, and press.

2 Place the batting on a flat surface; position the backing fabric right side up on top; and pin the two layers together. Cut to match the shape of the assembled hanger sections. Pin one border strip, right side up, to each long edge of the backing fabric and batting, with the decorative edge facing inward. Right sides together, pin the hanger section to the backing.

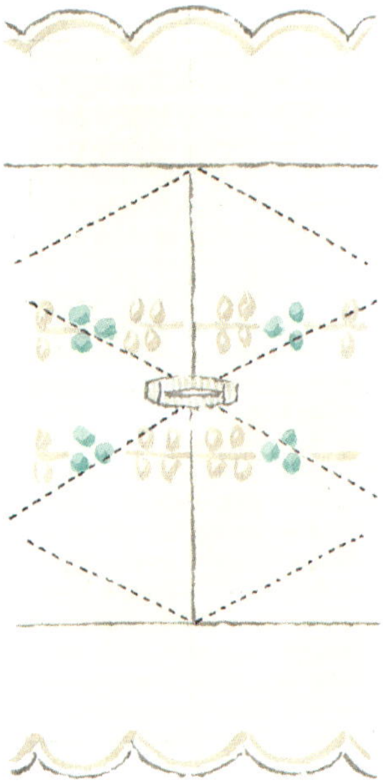

5 Make a 1-inch buttonhole in the center of the hanger front, crossing the center seam and working through all layers. (See page 119.) The buttonhole will correspond with the hole that you cut out of the batting in step 3.

6 Right sides together, fold the hanger cover in half lengthwise, and pin the curved outer ends together. Machine-stitch them together, taking a ½-inch seam. Turn right side out. Make three evenly spaced buttonholes on the front border, and stitch a button to correspond with each one on the border underneath. Decorate the base of the hook with an embroidered motif or ribbon bow. Place the cover over the hanger, threading the hook through the buttonhole at the center, and fasten the buttons on the border to secure.

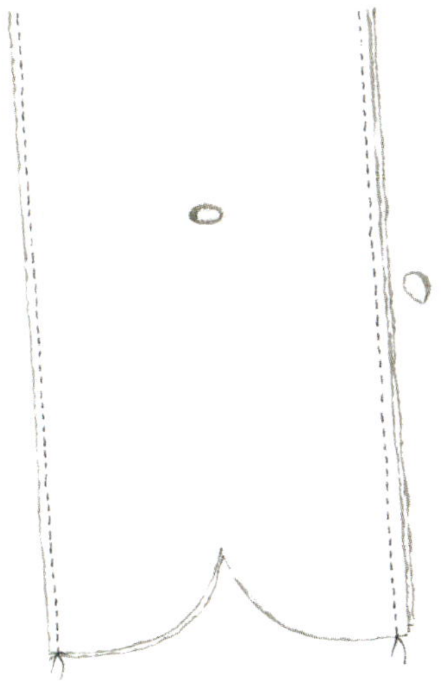

3 Stitch along both long edges, taking a ½-inch seam. Cut a tiny hole in the center of the batting, and remove a 1-inch oval of batting.

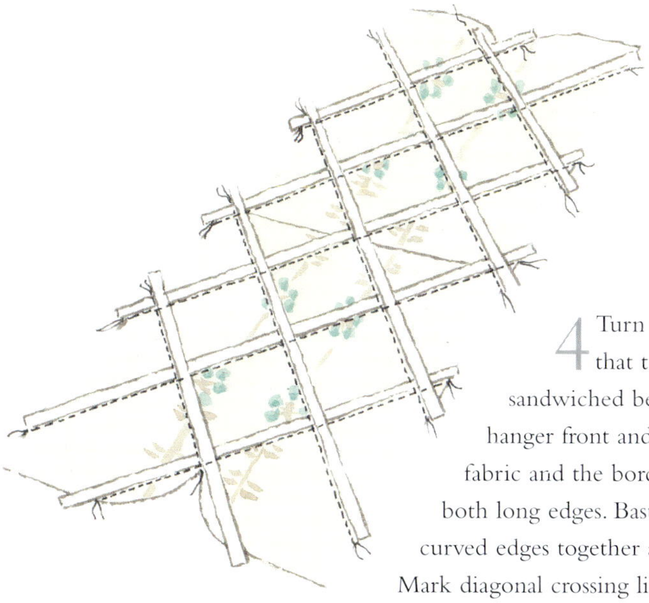

4 Turn right side out so that the batting is sandwiched between the hanger front and the backing fabric and the border is free along both long edges. Baste the raw curved edges together at both ends. Mark diagonal crossing lines over the hanger cover, using strips of masking tape to guide you. (See page 117). Quilt the hanger cover by machine or by hand. (See page 118.)

For a simple way of brightening up the base of the hook, cut around the edge of a satin-stitched embroidery motif with a pair of sharp, fine-pointed fabric scissors.

Techniques

The quilting craft has been practiced for centuries and has a rich made-by-hand tradition. Nowadays, few people have the time to make a quilt the old-fashioned way. However, achieving the one-of-a-kind look of something that is hand-made is still highly desirable.

In this book, the efficiency and speed of the sewing machine are used to make modern projects that look every bit as charming as their traditional, hand-sewn predecessors. All of the projects are pieced using a standard sewing machine. Some are finished with a small amount of hand-stitching, but this can also be done by machine. Straight lines of machine quilting can give a manufactured look if used excessively, and for smaller projects, a small amount of hand-finishing won't take long to complete.

The following pages provide an introduction to the equipment and techniques you need to make your own machine quilts and heirloom pieces.

EQUIPMENT

THE SEWING MACHINE

Even the most basic sewing machine can be used for machine quilting. Piecing patchwork together requires only a straight machine stitch. Most modern machines are now equipped to work zigzag stitching, which is particularly useful for quilting with bartacks or for finishing raw edges.

The basic foot that comes with the machine is fine for most of the jobs and can be used when doing patchwork. You will also need a piping or zipper foot for sewing piping or bulky braid into seams around pillows or handbags and totes, and for setting a zipper into a seam opening. A special quilting foot, which moves over thick fabrics easily, is available but it isn't essential. In addition to the standard throat plate, a gauge or adjustable spacer is a useful additional tool; it has a thin bar that sits horizontal to the quilt and is fixed above the machine foot to help keep spaces between parallel lines of stitching even. If the foot plate isn't marked with the required seam width, you can use a strip of masking tape to provide a guide line for making seam allowances accurate and consistent.

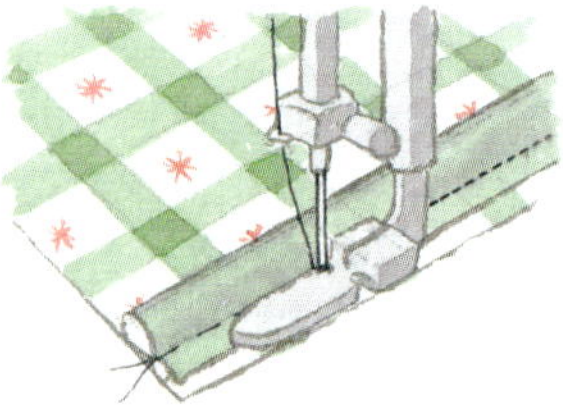

PIPING OR ZIPPER FOOT

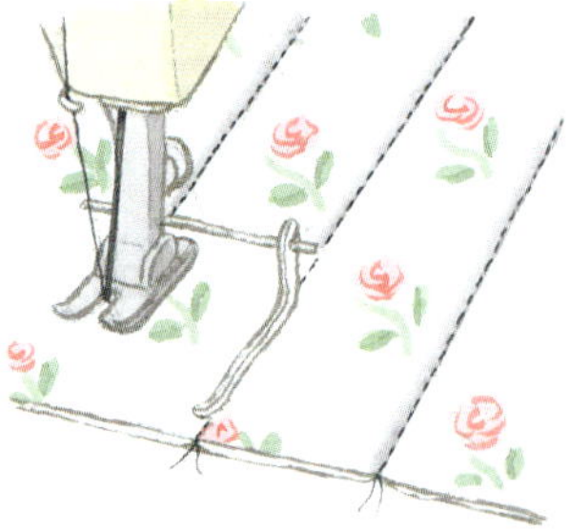

QUILTING FOOT WITH SPACER

OTHER BASIC SEWING TOOLS

Apart from a few special items, most of the tools you need for quilting fit into the general sewing category and will probably already be part of your sewing kit. Keep the equipment that you need for quilting in one place, so that it is easy to find and stays in good condition.

Thread

Use good-quality sewing thread for piecing the projects and No. 40 cotton or polyester-covered cotton thread for quilting. You can also buy special thread for hand quilting. Pulling lengths of thread through beeswax prior to stitching also helps to make the stitching smooth when working by hand.

Scissors

You will need three pairs—dressmaker's shears that you keep really sharp and use only for cutting fabric, general-purpose scissors for cutting paper pattern pieces, and sharp embroidery scissors for clipping threads and seam allowances.

Pins

To hold fabrics together while piecing patchwork, use fine dressmaker's pins that slide easily through the fabric. Glass-headed pins are the easiest to handle. Safety pins are useful for "pin-basting" layers of fabric together and will prevent you from scratching your hands when you're working with a bulky quilt. Use safety pins that are large enough to push comfortably through three layers without bunching or marking the fabrics.

Thimble

A thimble is useful for the small amounts of hand-stitching. A special quilting thimble has a flat top.

Iron

Always press seams open and flat as you go. It is well worth the trouble and helps to create a neat professional finish. When using fine fabrics through which the seams may show, you may need to press seams over to one side. "Pressing" in patchwork and quilting means precisely that. Press the iron down onto the fabric and then lift it up again, without dragging it over the material. Otherwise, you may stretch the fabric. Press carefully, using the point of the iron to reach into the seam and the flat of the iron to flatten the fabric.

Seam ripper

An essential tool for removing machine-made stitches quickly.

Rotary cutter and mat

An excellent tool for cutting the strips and straight-sided pieces for patchwork, a rotary cutter enables you to cut through several layers of fabric at the same time. Cutters and mats are available in different sizes; choose a medium-size cutter for general use. The blade must be razor sharp and handled with care. Always keep the protective cover over the blade when it is not in use. The cutter should only be used with a special self-healing cutting mat.

Rotary ruler

For use with a rotary cutter, a rotary ruler is made of thick, clear plastic and is marked with straight lines and angles.

Dressmaker's ruler or quilter's quarter

Needed for marking accurate seam allowances, a dressmaker's ruler is marked with a grid of lines. A quilter's quarter is a small square plastic ruler that is ¼ inch thick on all sides. Use it to check that seam allowances are even.

Marking pencils and chalk

You will need erasable pencils or quilter's pencils to mark fabric temporarily. Choose colors that are as close to your chosen fabric color as possible. Dressmaker's chalk pencils can also be used for the same purpose and will brush away later.

Pattern paper

Pattern paper marked with horizontal and vertical lines makes drawing pattern pieces easier.

USING A ROTARY CUTTER

A rotary cutter really helps to speed up the job of cutting out patchwork pieces and can give very accurate results. It is a particularly efficient way of cutting out strips of fabric; the strips, in turn, can be cut into squares and the squares into triangles.

Turn the fabric so that the rotary ruler covers the desired area. Using either the rotary ruler or the markings on the cutting mat, measure the width of the piece you are going to cut, and cut strips of this width along the grain of the fabric.

CUTTING STRIPS

BATTING AND INTERLININGS

A soft layer of padded material needs to be sandwiched inside a quilt and is usually referred to as batting ("wadding" in the UK). Quilting suppliers should have a range of batting made of cotton, wool, or synthetic material in a variety of widths and weights from which to choose.

Quilters often choose a thick batting when they first begin to quilt, because they are aiming for a more accentuated padded effect. With experience, you will probably find that lighter-weight battings are more attractive. A thinner fabric is easier to stitch through when hand-quilting, but machine quilts can be thicker. By the time the front and backing fabrics are added to the batting, even a fine interlining will produce a substantial finished effect.

Polyester batting

Polyester batting is probably the cheapest choice. It is available in several widths—39, 60, and 90 inches—and comes in a range of weights—usually 2, 3, 5, and 8 ounces. A good polyester batting will have crisp, lofty edges that you can butt together when joining widths for larger quilting projects.

Cotton batting

More-expensive cotton batting is usually 45 or 90 inches wide and 2 or 4 ounces in weight. Pre-wash cotton batting by hand before you use it, to pre-shrink the fabrics. Some people wait to wash the completed project instead, to give the quilt an antique, wrinkled look. However, this effect only happens when there are a lot of pieces that have been quilted close together.

Other types of quilt filling

Ready-cut pieces of batting to fit particular bed sizes are available from specialty suppliers and are referred to as quilting bats. Other alternatives for quilt fillings include domette (a woven cotton interlining that is often used as interlining in curtains and is especially useful for quilted wallhangings), cotton flannel, and lightweight blanket fabric. When making a bed quilt or throw, wide batting made for this specific purpose is the best choice for the padded layer. For smaller projects, you can use any interlining fabric. When interlining is specified in the project materials, you can use whatever filling you have on hand, but if the item will require laundering, pre-wash the filling layer beforehand.

FABRICS

Fabrics used for quilting should be pre-washed and checked for colorfastness before use. As a rule, pure cotton fabrics handle and wear well and are most suitable for larger bed quilts. You can use other fabrics, depending on how much wash and wear they will have to withstand. Consider the use of the finished quilt and choose your fabrics accordingly. Old silk and rayon ties, such as those used for the sewing-basket project on page 94, are unlikely to need laundering, but they might not be an appropriate choice for a bed quilt. Linen and fine woollen fabrics also work well for smaller pieces or accessories, and should always be pre-washed.

Use similar-weight fabrics together and consider the colors, shades and tones, and scale of the patterns. Small-scale patterns look like solid colors when seen from a distance, but they add texture to a design. Vary these elements within a project and use a range of color values. For some quilting block patterns, placing the correct tonal values within the pattern makes a big difference in how the pattern appears, as light-, medium-, and darker-toned fabrics in combination can create diagonal effects and shaded boxes throughout a design.

Backing fabric

Backing fabric can be either simple white or cream-color cotton or a colorful pattern in its own right. If a quilt will be seen on both sides, consider using a color or a patterned fabric that will complement or contrast with the quilt front.

TEMPLATES

Make templates for all of the pattern pieces in a project before you cut out the fabric patches. When the required pieces are squares and right-angled triangles, you can cut them without using a template, using a rotary cutter. Accuracy is of prime importance when making templates. Slight discrepancies will be magnified over an entire item and can result in patchwork that is misshapen.

Templates for machine sewing should have a ¼-inch seam allowance on all edges. Trace them onto pattern paper; then cut out the paper shapes. Templates that will be used again should be cut from cardboard or special template plastic, so they will be more robust.

To make your own templates from a quilting block plan, copy the outlines of the pieces and then add a ¼-inch seam allowance to all of the edges. Position the straight edge of a pattern piece to follow the grain of the fabric.

JOINING THE PATCHWORK PIECES

Many patchwork patterns are designed as blocks, which can be either repeated or joined to other sections.

Pattern pieces for machine quilting should be be simple geometric shapes—rectangles, squares, triangles, or diamonds—with straight sides that can easily be joined into blocks or combined with strips to make a larger piece. Avoid curves and angles.

Join pieces by placing straight edges right sides together, and stitch with a ¼-inch seam. Press seams as you go.

Chain piecing

To save on sewing thread and time, construct groups of fabric pieces at the same time, running them through the machine one after the other without cutting the threads between each one.

Place pairs of fabric together, and feed them through the machine without lifting the foot or breaking the thread, letting the machine take two or three stitches at the end of one unit before you feed in the next one. When you have pieced the required number of units, cut through the threads between the units.

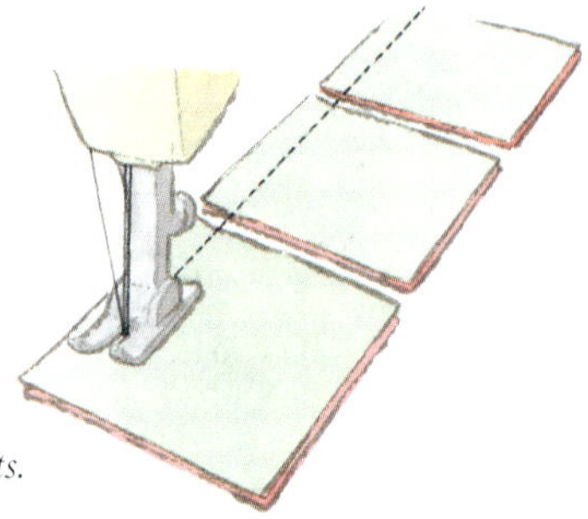

CHAIN PIECING

LAYERING THE FABRICS

There are two main ways of assembling the different layers of fabric for a quilt. The first way is to lay out the quilt backing right side down, with the batting on top of it, and the quilt top (right side up) on top of the batting. This way will leave the edges of the quilt raw and you will have to cover them with a binding.

The second method, which is known as "bagging," gives a quilt a neat finished edge that will not require binding.

BAGGING THE QUILT

Place the quilt front right side up on top of the baiting and the backing fabric right side down on top of the quilt front. Stitch a ½-inch seam around the edges, leaving an opening in one of the seams that is big enough through which to turn the quilt. Turn the quilt to the right side, and flatten the fabrics out. Turn under the opening edges, and slip-stitch the opening closed. Press the edges. Pin and baste the layers together prior to quilting.

Whichever method you choose, the fabrics must be pinned or basted together so that they will stay together securely and all the layers can be treated as one.

Smooth out the layers with your hands. Working from the center outward, make large basting stitches through all layers. Fastening safety pins through the layers is another good way of securing the fabrics across the quilt—and it protects your hands from sharp pins as you manipulate the quilt.

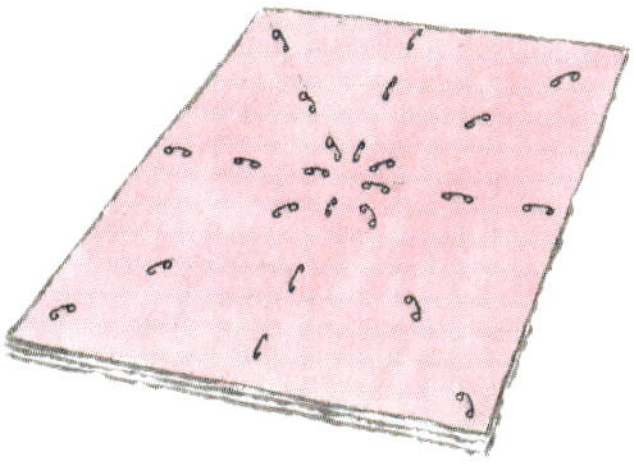

ASSEMBLING THE QUILT LAYERS

MACHINE QUILTING

The layers of fabric that form a quilt must be held together in a permanent way. Different battings dictate how close together these joins need to be. The quilting can be stitched by machine or hand, knotted, or buttoned. Bartacks can be made on the sewing machine or decorative rosettes can be stitched at regular intervals through all of the layers.

To mark the position of straight or intersecting lines of stitching across a quilt, press strips of low-tack masking tape lightly against the fabric to provide a guide and keep your stitching neat.

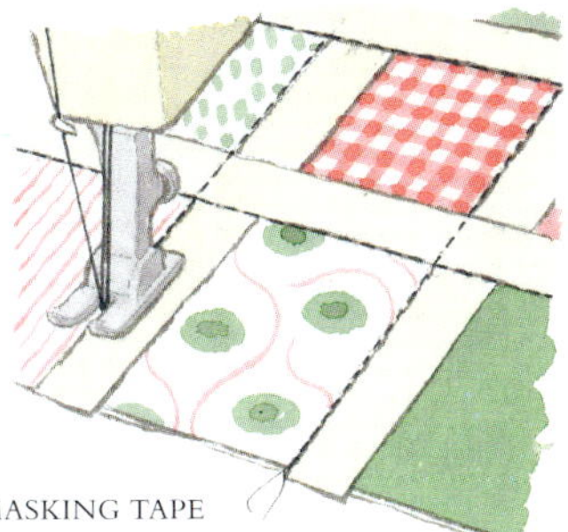

USING MASKING TAPE TO MAKE GUIDE LINES

Before beginning a new project, insert a new needle (size 14 or 12 is recommended for the medium-weight fabrics used in this book). The stitch needs to be slightly longer than for regular sewing, so loosen the tension slightly and set the stitch length to 12 stitches per 1 inch. A walking, even feed is essential to prevent tucks from forming in the quilt top or backing. To begin and end a line of stitching, change the stitch length and work seven or eight very short stitches and then cut off the loose threads close to the quilt.

Quilting large items

The larger the quilt, the more difficult it is to manipulate under the sewing machine. Work from the center of the quilt outward, rolling up the edges of the quilt under the machine as you go. This is why it is important that you pin or baste the layers securely so that they do not shift out of position while you are moving the quilt around.

Roll up the quilt and secure it with clips or pins so that you can work on a small section at a time.

MANIPULATING THE FABRIC

Types of machine quilting

In addition to straight runs of machine stitches in parallel lines or intersected lines to make a lattice design, machine quilting can be worked to create other effects. Begin and end lines of stitching with a few short close-together stitches, trimming the thread ends as close to the quilt as possible. Alternatively, pull the ends of threads on the top through to the back of the quilt; thread through a needle; and overstitch a few times to secure. Trim ends close to the quilt.

Ditch quilting is when the quilt is stitched through all of the layers, following the groove of a seam. The line of stitching will disappear into the seam and will be virtually invisible.

DITCH QUILTING

Contour quilting is when lines of stitching are sewn within a patchwork shape to give an even raised border inside the shape. The effect is a bold, sculptural quality.

CONTOUR QUILTING

HAND QUILTING

In traditional hand quilting, parallel lines of small running stitches were used to make the quilting. This method still has a charming look, but it can take a long time to do. However, there are also some simple ways of holding the layers together that do not require lots of stitching.

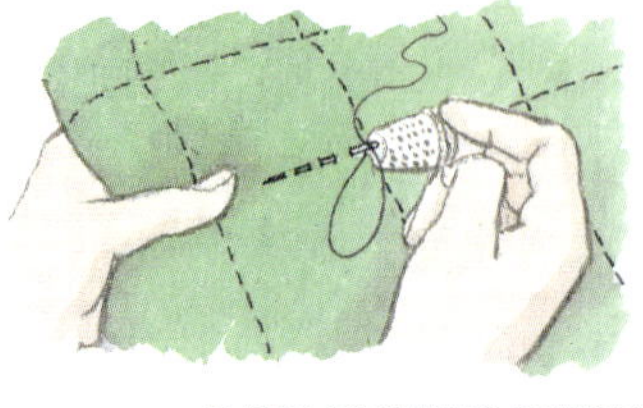

HAND QUILTING STITCH

Quilt with running stitches worked in and out through the layers. Wear a thimble on the middle finger of your sewing hand to push the needle through, and use your thumb to push the fabric down in front of the stitches. The index finger of the other hand underneath the quilt can push the needle back up to the right side. With a bit of practice you can make a few stitches at a time, repeatedly going up and down through the fabrics. Aim for approximately six stitches per inch.

Tied quilting

Embroidery thread stitched through the layers can be knotted on the right side of the quilt to make a small tuft. Repeated over the quilt at regular intervals, this is an effective and quick method of quilting the layers together.

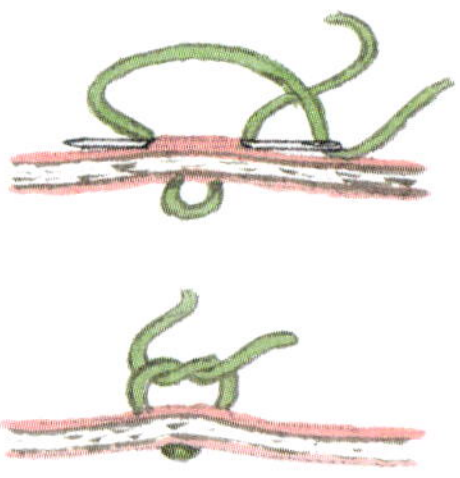

KNOTTING THREADS

Start the knot on the right side of the quilt so that the end of the thread is long enough to tie, and make a ¼-inch stitch, working two or three times through the layers and ending with the thread on the right side. Tie the ends with a flat knot, and trim the ends evenly. For fluffier tufts, make the first half of the knot and then lay a few threads centrally across the half knot and finish the knot over them. Cut all of the ends to the same length.

Rosettes and buttons

Fabric rosettes, felt mattress washers, and buttons can all be useful methods of quilting. Fabric-covered buttons made using scraps of embroidered fabric are wonderful decorations. Use fragments of embroidered mats for this purpose. Stitch fabric rosettes securely in place through all of the layers.

BINDING

Quilt edges can be finished with deep borders or with narrow binding. Straight edges can be bound with straight strips of fabric, cut on the grain. To bind curves you will need to use bias binding, which is cut diagonally.

Bias strips can be cut individually from fabric but can be wasteful because they stretch diagonally across the fabric. To join strips, place right sides together matching slanted edges, as shown, and stitch with a ¼-inch seam. Press the seam open.

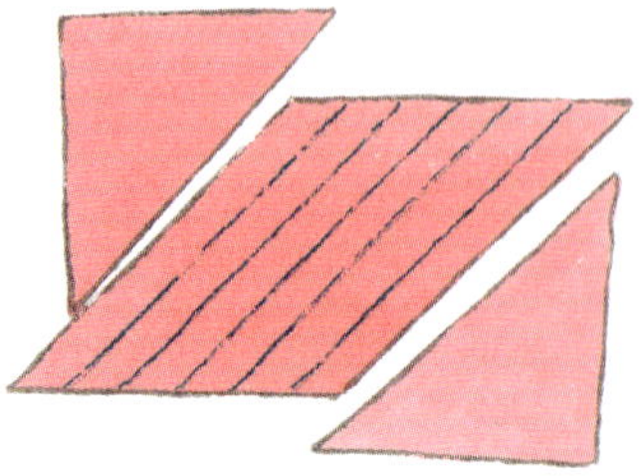

CUTTING OUT THE BIAS STRIPS

1. For a continuous strip, cut out a rectangle of fabric that is at least twice as long as it is wide. Fold the top right-hand corner over, so that the top edge runs down the left-hand side edge of the rectangle to make a right-angled triangle. Press the fold and cut off the triangle along the fold. Right sides together and taking a ¼-inch seam, stitch the triangle to the other end of the rectangle, as shown. Press the seam open.

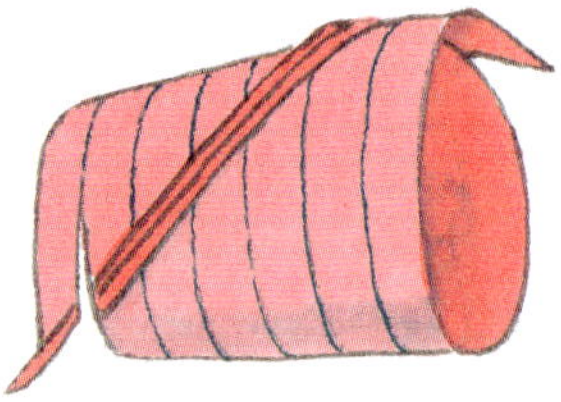

CUTTING A CONTINUOUS STRIP

2. Working down and across the right side of the fabric, mark slanted parallel lines to fit the required width of the bias strips. Number the rows, staggering the numbers so that the first row on the left is 1, the first row on the right is 2, the second row on the left is 2, and so on. Fold the piece with right sides together, and stitch to join the numbered edges, matching the numbers (2 to 2, 3 to 3, and so on) to make a tube. Press the seam open. Turn to the right side. Starting from the top, cut along the ruled lines to make a continuous strip.

PIPING

Piping gives a tailored finish to edges of pillows and bags. When piping cord is used, the seams turn out in a very stylish and even way. You can use store-bought piping or make your own to match or complement the main fabric.

Piping cord

To make piping, fold a bias-cut strip of fabric over the piping cord so that long edges meet and wrong sides are together. Using a piping foot, stitch close to the cord through both layers of fabric.

When stitching piping into a seam, join the ends where they meet. Unpick the stitching along the one end of piping cord for about 1 inch. Cut the cord so that both ends butt next to each other. Cut the fabric so that it overlaps by about ½ inch. Fold under ¼ inch to the wrong side and overlap this folded edge over the other end to cover the raw edge. Stitch in place to join the ends.

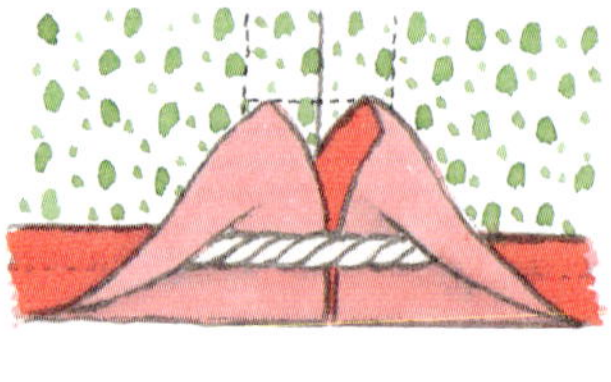

PIPING CORD

MITERING CORNERS

Mitered corners give a professional finish to borders and bound edges. The fabric is folded over to meet at the corner so the seam line is exactly mid way between both side edges.

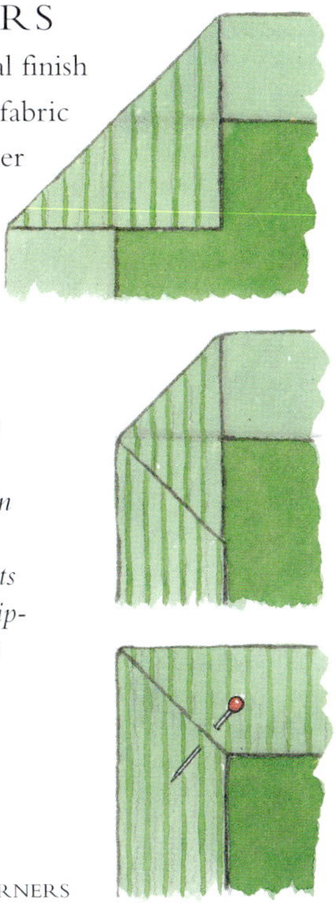

Fold in a small hem of equal depth on both sides of the fabric, and press. Fold the corner so that the straight outside edge that it forms is at a right angle to the midway line between the side edges. Fold the side edges in again so that the straight outer edge on the corner splits exactly into two and meets down the middle. Pin in place, and slip-stitch or machine-topstitch close to the folded edge to secure. Slip-stitch the mitered edges together to complete.

MITERING CORNERS

INSERTING A ZIPPER

Right sides together, pin the two pieces that are to be joined by a zipper and, taking a ½-inch seam, machine-stitch for 2½ inches in from each edge so that the center of the seam is open. Turn under the seam allowances along both sides of the opening. With the right side up, pin and then baste a zipper into the opening. Machine-stitch the zipper in place using a zipper foot on the machine.

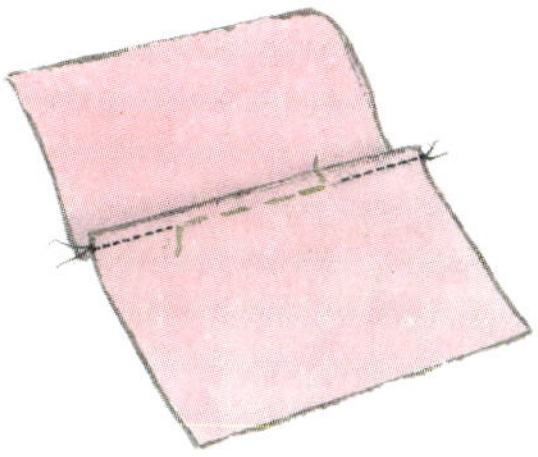

INSERTING A ZIPPER

USEFUL HAND STITCHES

Even when you are making things using a sewing machine, there are always times when you are called upon to do a few hand stitches—usually to secure a hem or to close openings at the sides of folded borders so that the stitches are invisible. Simple embroidery stitches are also useful for finishing touches with an unmistakable handmade look.

When securing hems or closing openings in seams, use small slip-stitches to join folded edges together or to a single layer of fabric. Slide the needle through the fold and then back through the lower fabric, making small, evenly spaced stitches.

SLIP STITCH

French knots make an attractive raised dot. Bring the needle up through the fabric to where you want the knot. With the needle pointing away from you, twist the thread once around the needle (or twice to make a larger knot). Twist the needle around so that the point goes into the fabric directly beside where it originally emerged. Keeping the thread taut, push the needle back through to the back of the fabric. The knot will form on the top of the fabric.

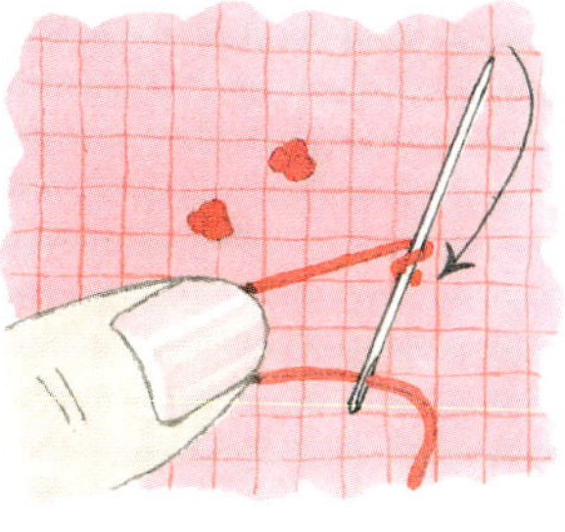

FRENCH KNOT

BUTTONHOLES

Make buttonholes following the instructions that come with your machine. Buttonholes are always made of two lines of narrow, closely spaced zigzag lines of stitching with a wide bartack across both ends. The groove between the two lines is then slit open using a seam ripper.

MAKING A PILLOW

Right sides facing, pin the two back pieces together, and stitch a ½-inch seam 2 inches in from both ends so that the center of the seam is open to fit the length of the zipper. Turn under the seam allowances along both sides of the opening. With the right side up, pin a zipper into the opening, and machine-stitch in place using a zipper foot. Open the zipper; then with right sides facing, pin the pillow front to the back, and stitch a ½-inch seam around the edges. Neaten the raw edges with a zigzag machine stitch. Turn to the right side, and press seamed edges flat.

CARE, STORAGE, AND WASHING

If you have used good-quality materials and tested them for colorfastness, a hand-made quilt should give years of service. The ideal place to store a quilt is on an unused bed if you have one, away from bright sunlight and fluorescent light. Quilts look wonderful piled high in linen cupboards with wire mesh see-through doors, but make sure that light does not fade the areas of quilt in view and that dust does not mark the folds. If you need to store a quilt long term, fold it and place it in an acid-free box or a 100-percent white-cotton pillowcase with crumpled acid-free tissue paper in the folds. If it fits comfortably inside a washing machine, a small quilt with synthetic batting can be machine-washed in warm water using a mild detergent. Tumble dry on a low setting—or, better still, dry it flat. Wash large quilts gently by hand in a bathtub using mild detergent, and rinse it until the water runs clear. Press the quilt gently with your hands to remove excess water; then press thick towels on the quilt to soak up as much water as possible. Dry it flat on dry towels in a warm place, out of direct sunlight.

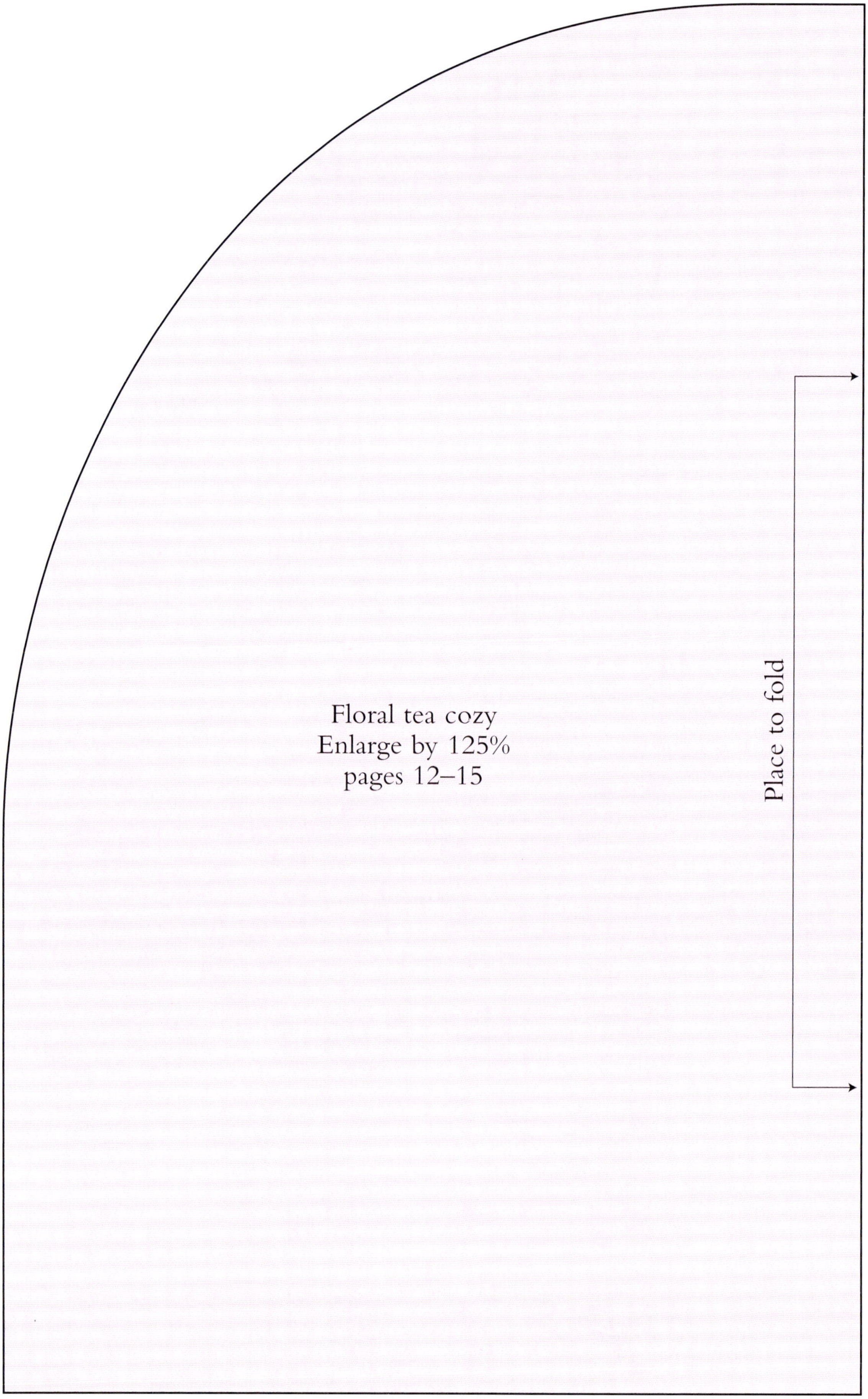
Floral tea cozy
Enlarge by 125%
pages 12–15
Place to fold

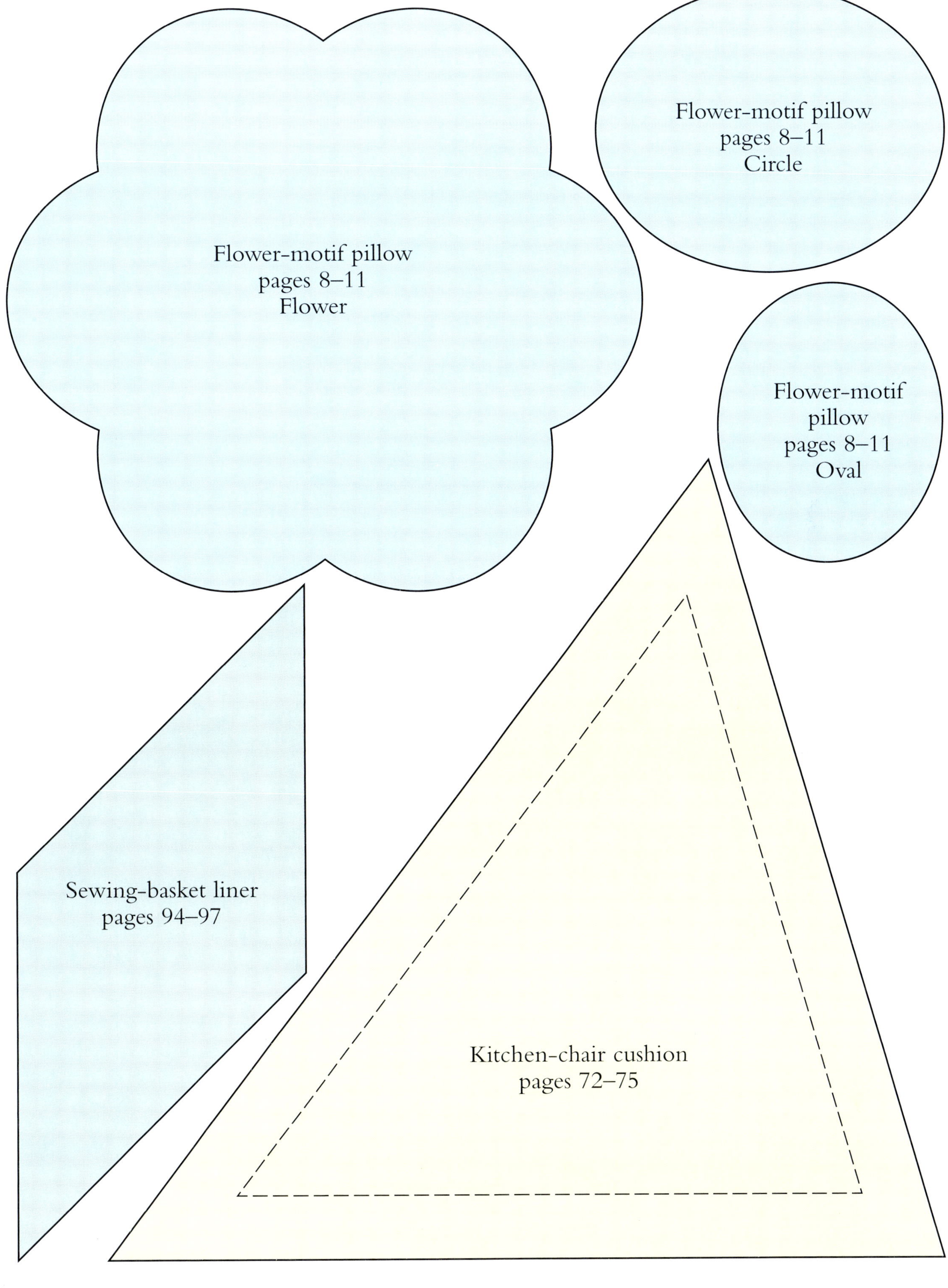
Flower-motif pillow
pages 8–11
Flower
Flower-motif pillow
pages 8–11
Circle
Flower-motif pillow
pages 8–11
Oval
Sewing-basket liner
pages 94–97
Kitchen-chair cushion
pages 72–75

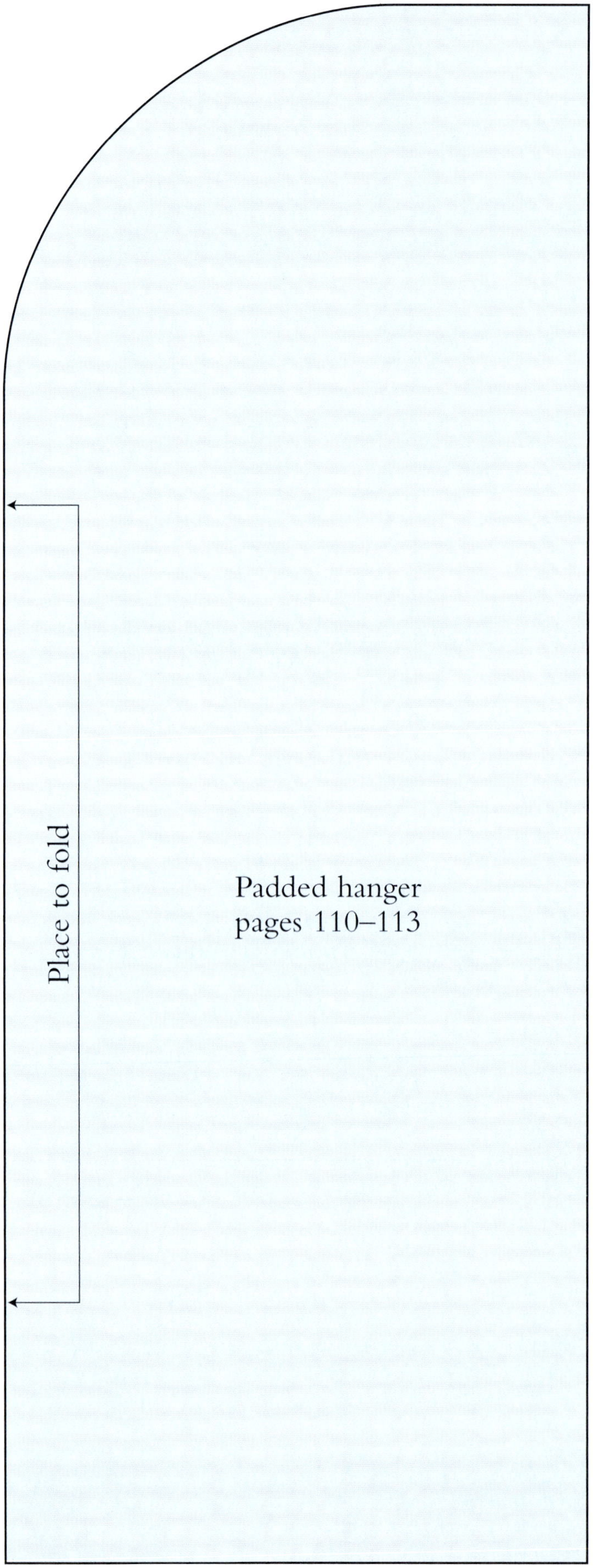
Place to fold
Padded hanger
pages 110–113

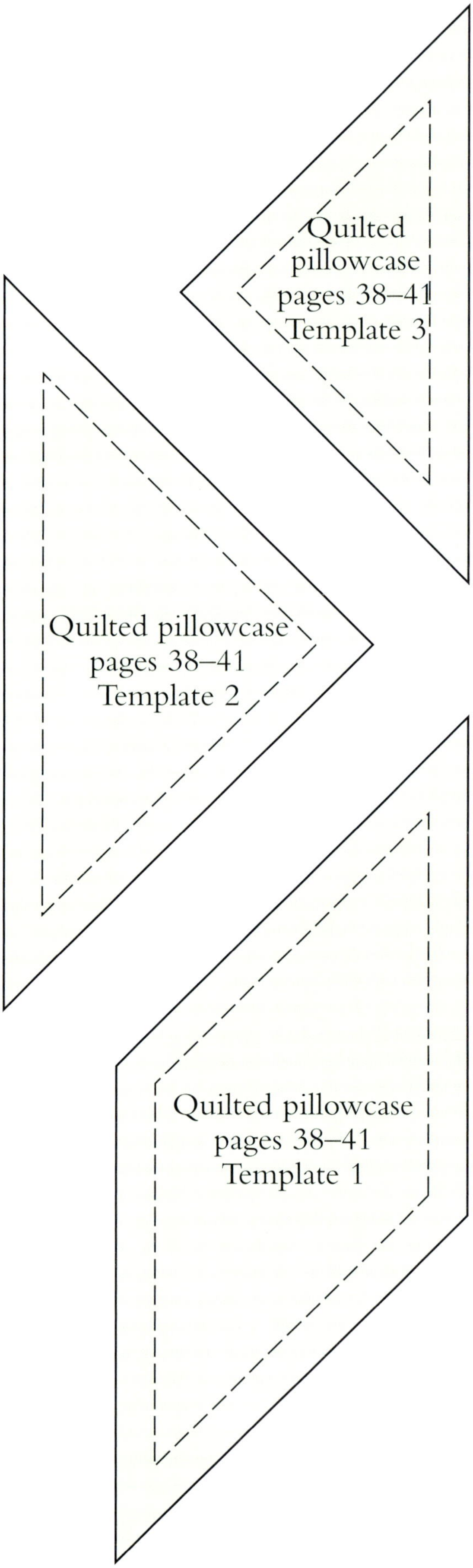
Quilted
pillowcase
pages 38–41
Template 3
Quilted pillowcase
pages 38–41
Template 2
Quilted pillowcase
pages 38–41
Template 1

Polka-dot tablecloth
pages 24–27
Template 4

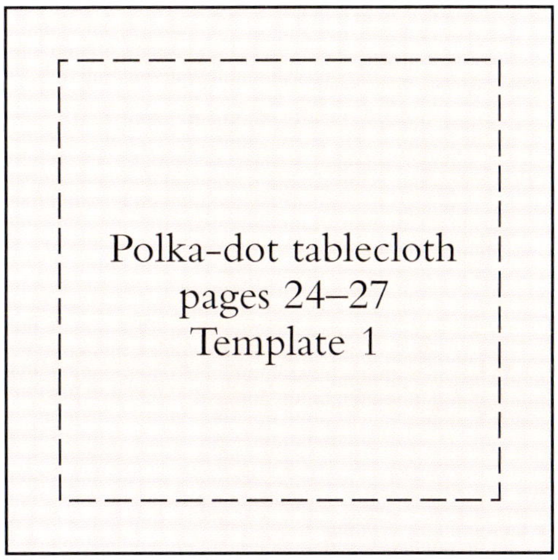
Polka-dot tablecloth
pages 24–27
Template 1

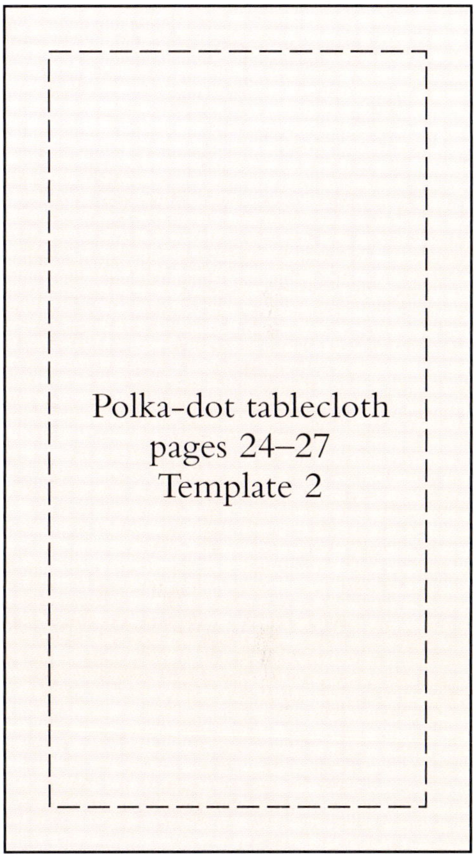
Polka-dot tablecloth
pages 24–27
Template 2

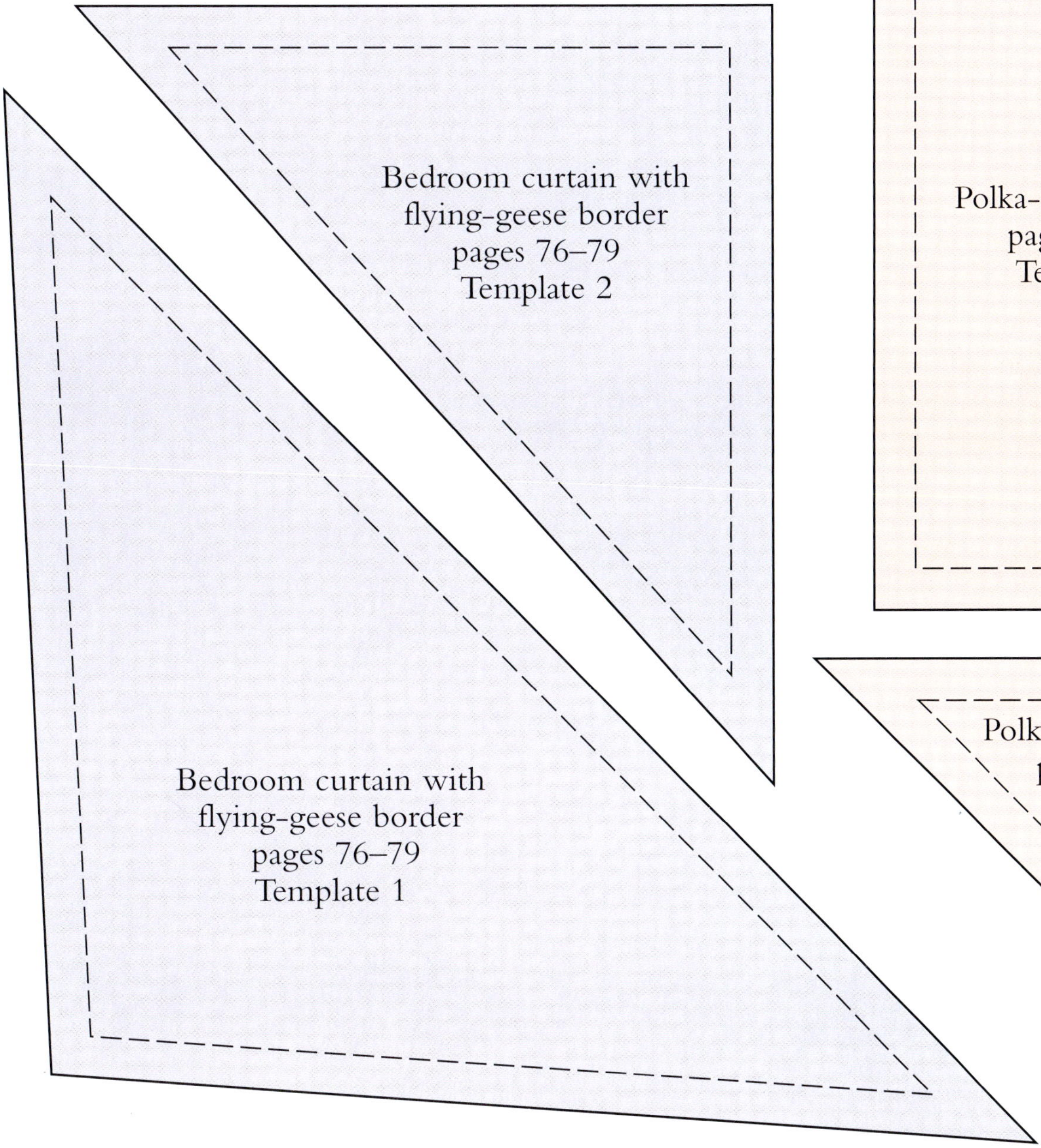
Bedroom curtain with
flying-geese border
pages 76–79
Template 2
Bedroom curtain with
flying-geese border
pages 76–79
Template 1

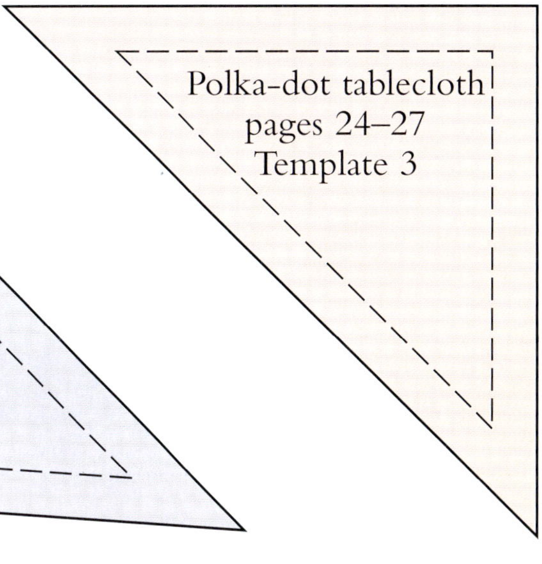
Polka-dot tablecloth
pages 24–27
Template 3

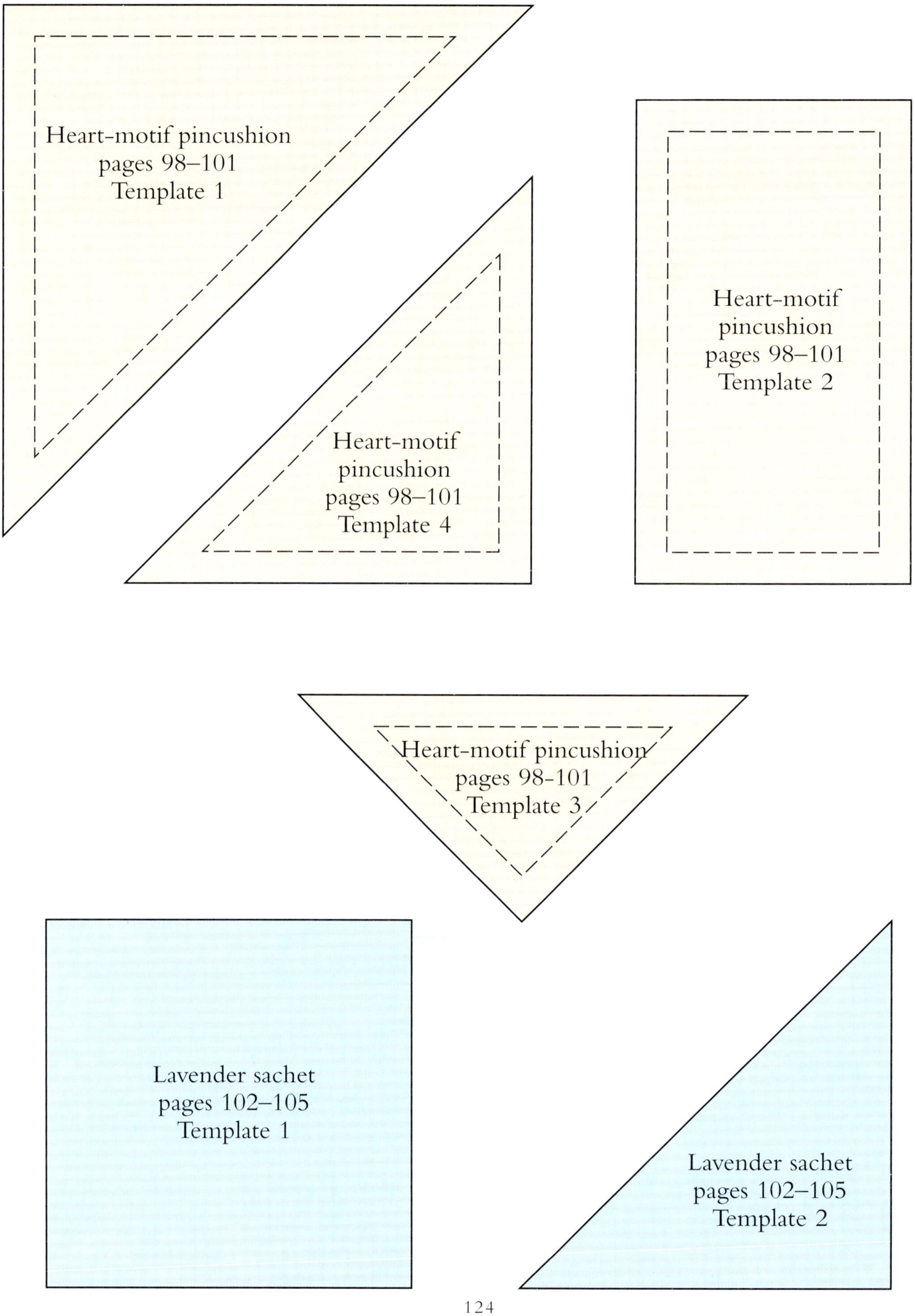
Heart-motif pincushion
pages 98–101
Template 1
Heart-motif pincushion
pages 98–101
Template 4
Heart-motif pincushion
pages 98–101
Template 2
Heart-motif pincushion
pages 98-101
Template 3
Lavender sachet
pages 102–105
Template 1
Lavender sachet
pages 102–105
Template 2

Star-patterned laundry bag
pages 106–109
Template 1

Star-patterned laundry bag
pages 106–109
Template 4

Star-patterned
laundry bag
pages 106–109
Template 5

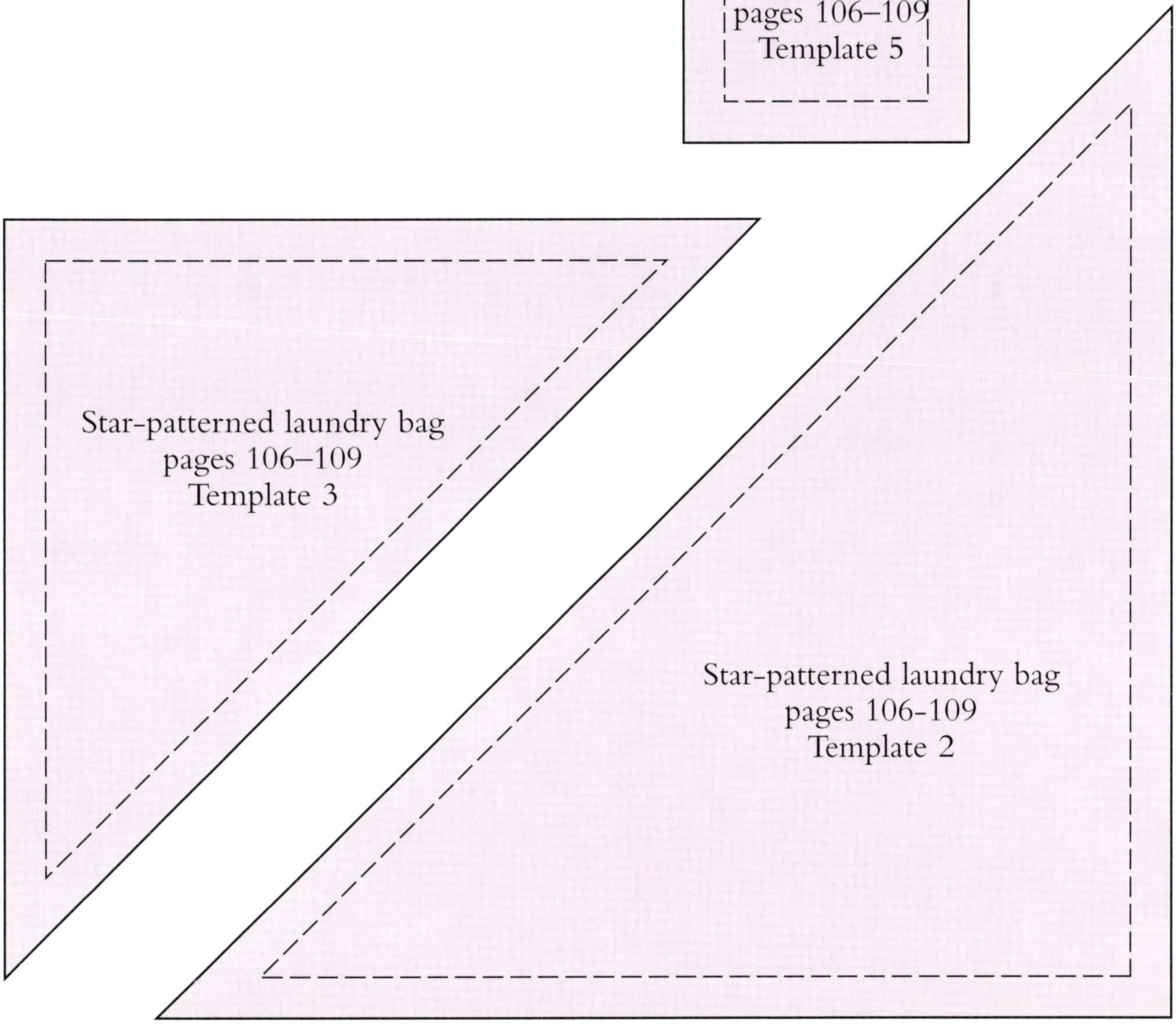
Star-patterned laundry bag
pages 106–109
Template 3
Star-patterned laundry bag
pages 106-109
Template 2

Bed throw
pages 50–53

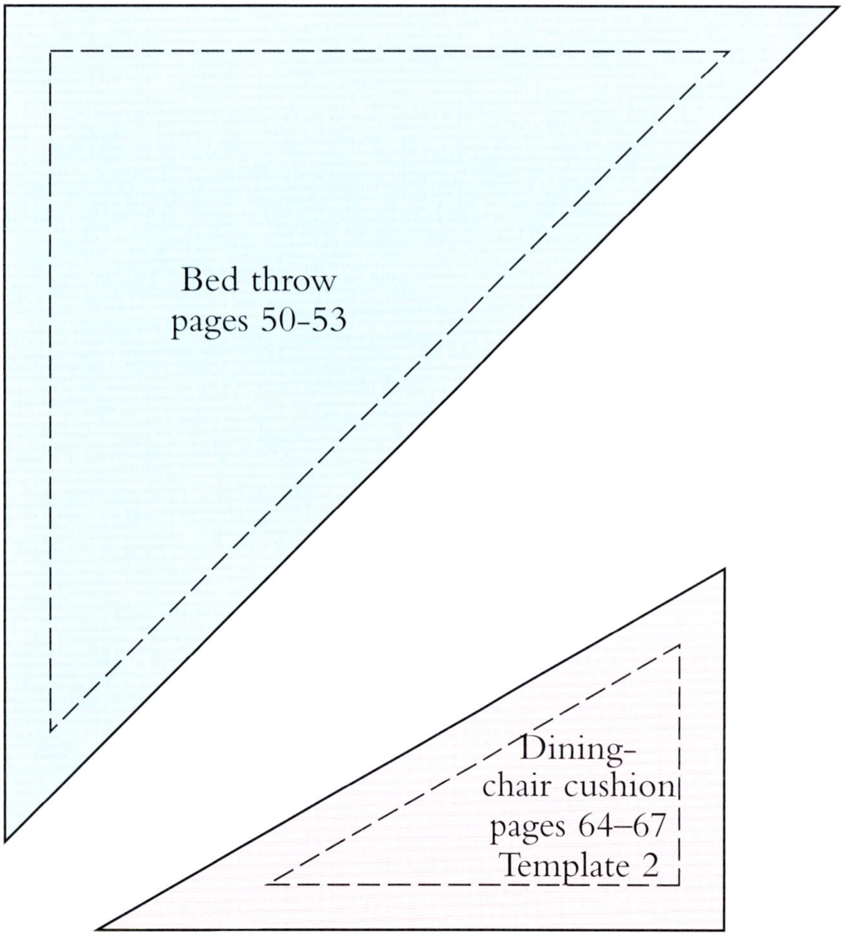
Bed throw
pages 50-53
Dining-
chair cushion
pages 64–67
Template 2

Dining-chair cushion
pages 64–67
Template 5

Dining-chair cushion
pages 64–67
Template 6

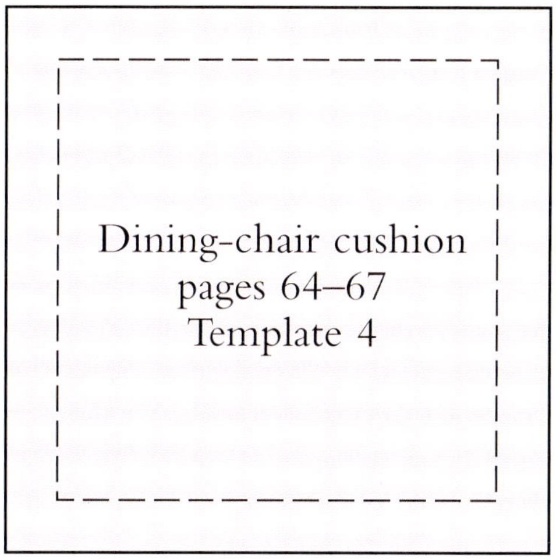
Dining-chair cushion
pages 64–67
Template 4

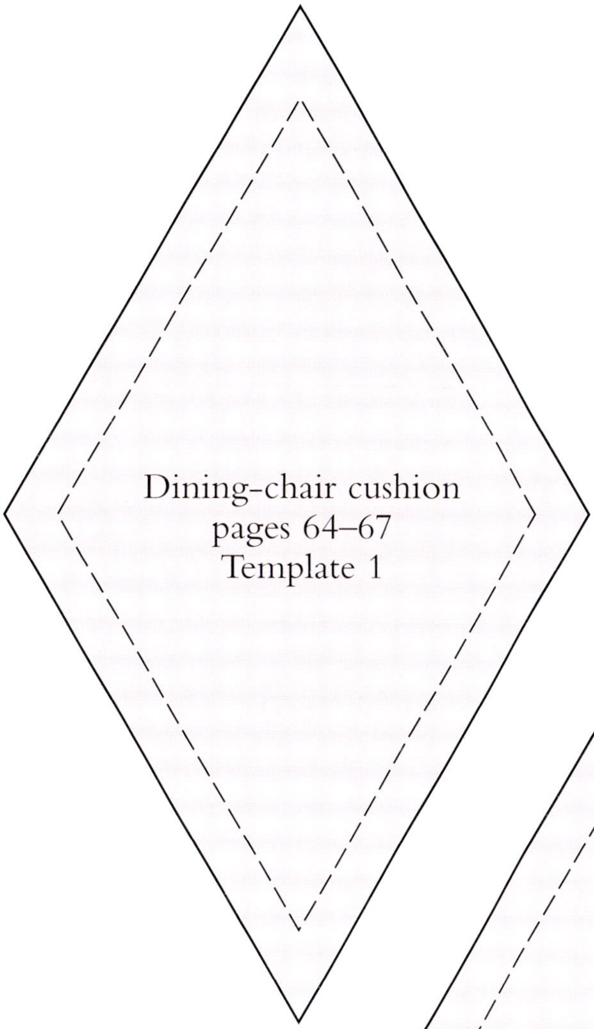
Dining-chair cushion
pages 64–67
Template 1

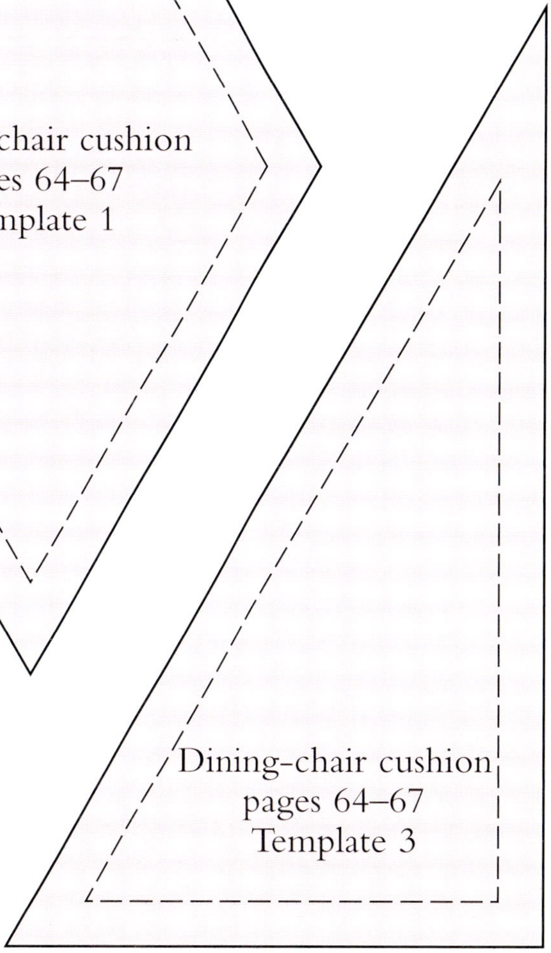
Dining-chair cushion
pages 64–67
Template 3